A CONCISE GUIDE TO GETTING GRANTS FOR NONPROFIT ORGANIZATIONS

A CONCISE GUIDE TO GETTING GRANTS FOR NONPROFIT ORGANIZATIONS

MARK GUYER

Kroshka Books
New York

Senior Editors: Susan Boriotti and Donna Dennis
Coordinating Editor: Tatiana Shohov
Office Manager: Annette Hellinger
Graphics: Wanda Serrano
Editorial Production: Jennifer Vogt, Matthew Kozlowski, Jonathan Rose
and Maya Columbus
Circulation: Ave Maria Gonzalez, Indah Pecker, Raymond Davis and Nicolas Miro
Communications and Acquisitions: Serge P. Shohov
Marketing: Cathy DeGregory

Library of Congress Cataloging-in-Publication Data
Available Upon Request

ISBN 1-59033-087-0.

Copyright © 2002 by Nova Science Publishers, Inc.
400 Oser Ave. Suite 1600
Hauppauge, New York 11788
Tele. 631-231-7269   Fax 631-231-8175
E Mail: Novascience@earthlink.net
www.novapublishers.com

Printed in the United States of America

DEDICATED TO MY MOTHER AND FATHER

Special Thanks Go To
Charles and Belva Schaffter
and Mary Hanna

CONTENTS

Chapter 1   First Steps   1

Chapter 2   Sources of Grants   9

Chapter 3   Finding the Information You Need   29

Chapter 4   How to Write an Effective Grant Request   55

Chapter 5   Conclusion   101

Appendix 1   Other Fund-Raising Options   105

Appendix 2   Internet Sites for Grant Seekers   121

Index   123

Chapter 1

FIRST STEPS

**"Opportunity is missed by most people because it is
dressed in overalls and looks like work."
Thomas Edison**

There are these three grant consultants. Each year they fly to the wild northern forests of Canada to camp and hunt moose. This last fall they went up again. A bush pilot flew them to their campsite in a small airplane with pontoons, landing on a lake, because no roads go there. After a week, he came back to pick the men up. Each consultant had gotten a moose and they all wanted to take the moose carcasses back as trophies. However, the pilot told them, "You know we can't possibly do that, it's too much weight." So, they got out their money and offered him $300. "No way," he said. "$400?" "No." "$500?" "No." By the time they got to $700, the pilot said, "Well... OK." They stuffed themselves, the moose, and all their camping gear into the tiny cabin of the airplane. There wasn't an inch of space left. The little Cessna taxied into position, then raced down the lake, bouncing along. Finally the airplane barely lifted off the blue water. But, it just didn't have enough altitude to rise above the first row of pine trees at the edge of the lake. The plane plowed right into the trees, though the trees cushioned the crash and no one was hurt. The contents of the plane were scattered all over. There were moose, men, and clothing hanging from the tree branches. One consultant looked over at another and asked, "Where are we? Where are we?" The other looked back and said, "I think we're about a hundred feet farther than where we crashed last year."

Does it seem that sometimes in life we just manage to crash about a hundred feet farther than last year? This guidebook has been written to help you so that doesn't happen with your grant requests. You will learn the fundamentals of getting grants. We will cover how the grant process works, finding a funder, sources of grant information, and writing a grant request (called a grant proposal).

When we consider the topic of grants, we are dealing with an important subject, we're talking money. There are substantial benefits for you in learning about grants. You can *get personal recognition*, *advance* in your job, *add variety* to your work, and *obtain a marketable skill*. Once you learn how to get grants you can get several a year. Your nonprofit organization, through your efforts, can secure funds for significant projects that help people. These benefits will be *of value through your whole career*.

As the recipients of grants, nonprofit organizations have key roles in the philanthropic system. Nonprofits meet the spectrum of human needs with grants. Nonprofit groups lift up people, causing those people to become stronger and better. You can be proud that you are dedicated to such goals. A grant is a method to increase your effectiveness in reaching your goals. A grant is money which does not need to be paid back.

The American system of grant making is remarkable. It allows our society to accomplish many valuable objectives which could not be accomplished otherwise. Many charitable foundations have been formed by persons who were fortunate enough to become wealthy, and who were wise enough to do something good with their wealth. Because of the charitable concerns of caring individuals our whole system of philanthropy exists, in which people give away money to help other people they have never met.

A few years ago men and women walking down a street were asked to define "philanthropy." There were answers such as "stamp collecting" and "the study of monkeys." Philanthropy is actually the promotion of human welfare by making monetary contributions, often in the form of grants.

THE GRANT PLAN

The first step in obtaining a grant is the development of a well thought-out plan to be funded. You need to have a clearly defined plan in mind before you can get very far. After those persons appropriately involved, including administrators, have agreed to the plan, then you are in a position to move forward. To receive a grant there should be readiness and consensus within your organization. In some situations you may want to include the group to be served in the planning process.

The most important factor in determining whether you get a positive response to your grant request is: how good the plan for the use of the grant really is. So you should spend time to fully develop the concept that forms the basis for the plan. You should have a concept that will be effective in producing significant outcomes. You have no doubt heard some ideas and plans where you work that were, shall we say, less than good. If the plan for the use of the grant is weak, then the results from the grant will be poor. Having a project worth doing is essential in getting support from a funder.

To get a grant it is necessary to have:

- A Good Plan
- A Good Funder
- A Good Proposal

There must be a grant plan deserving of support, sent to an appropriate funder, in a proposal that makes a strong case for the grant.

I was once in... let's call it "an unfortunate situation," where I was asked to help with getting a grant. After three years of sporadic efforts, the folks who wanted the grant still had not clearly decided what they would do with the grant. There was some contention about what to call the project. I have not heard anything from that group for quite awhile. As far as I know, the project has dissolved. I don't want to ask, because I'm hoping everyone has forgotten that I was ever involved with it.

People just starting to learn about grants usually assume that most of their efforts should go into writing the grant request. Experienced grant seekers spend more time on planning how the grant will be used. Yogi Berra reportedly once said, "You've got to be very careful if you don't know where you are going, because you might not get there."

> Choose an idea which will have appeal to a funding source. For example, it would be better to request money to fund a job search class for handicapped clients, than to seek funding for remodeling a reception room. The amounts may be the same, both are legitimate needs, however one has much more attractiveness to grant makers.

The plan for the use of the grant should be designed to achieve significant results. Grant makers tend to focus on what results their grant will purchase, which is understandable.

Many grant makers prefer to back new projects, rather than to provide basic operating costs. Some grant makers see operating costs as the responsibility of the nonprofit itself. Grantmakers desire to make a difference, and that more clearly happens when starting something new, instead of subsidizing what is already being done. So that is a factor to keep in mind.

Possibly you have an innovative program which could be planted in other communities. Demonstration projects or pilot programs to prove the effectiveness of new approaches carry the promise of benefits beyond just one location. If your new program can help in other cities that is an advantage.

Collaboration with other nonprofit organizations is a plus in winning a grant. Cooperating can make agencies more effective. Each group can bring its unique abilities into action. There is less likely to be duplication of effort. Collaboration is evidence of significant thought and planning. Many grant makers view proposals involving collaboration as stronger. Also, it is harder to turn down two or more groups than just one.

You may wish to make going for a grant into a team effort within your organization. Check around to find out if any of your co-workers have experience with grants. Several persons can divide the work into parts that way, and there is more than one perspective. Perhaps one person could locate funders and another one could write the grant proposal. If more than one person writes the grant proposal, it should have consistency and read as if one person wrote it.

One week a while ago, I had contacts with two nonprofits. On Tuesday I received a thank you letter from an organization for which I had served as a consultant. They got the grant they wanted and they were pleased. On Wednesday I went to a meeting at an organization which was faced with a funding deadline. Their proposal was due by the end of that week and they had not started it yet. They did not have a definite plan for the use of the grant. In fact they had only a few general ideas about what they would like to do.

The Tuesday group took the time to do things right. They studied the grants process. They did the research. They picked an appropriate funding source. They had a good idea with an effective plan. The Wednesday group jumped in late, slapped together a questionable plan, and then wrote a somewhat vague grant proposal covered up with slick wording. The Tuesday group got a grant. The Wednesday group did not. No surprise there. It pays, literally, to take the time to do things right.

One aspect of doing things right is learning about grants. The subject of grants may at first appear new and hard to understand. It may be a new topic to you right now, but it is not hard to understand. With a little time, grants will not seem new or hard to understand.

A dilemma I face in telling you about grants is that I do not want to make the topic of getting grants unnecessarily complex. But I do not want to leave out ideas that you might need to know about. So to be safe I have included more information than you may need.

As far as what you should remember, if you remember just the main points in this book you will do fine. **You can get a grant if you understand the basics**. The basics of getting a grant are easy to learn.

For your convenience, there is a short summary of the whole grant seeking process after this chapter. Please use this checklist. If ten minutes ago you had no idea of how to get a grant, you do now, follow this checklist. It will take you in proper sequence through what to do from start to finish.

In this book there is a work sheet for finding a funder, and a work sheet for writing a grant proposal. There is an example of a grant proposal. An eight section proposal format of proven effectiveness will be fully explained. I have used this format myself to get substantial grants.

There are many reference books and other resources which will assist you. There are books which tell about: individual foundations, grant making corporations, available government grants, who awards grants for needs like yours, and past grants that have been made. The best of these resources will be described in later pages.

As you read, put down on paper those points that you want to remember. Having those notes will help you. Please be aware that the Internet sites noted in the pages of this book are not repeated in the net list at the end of the book.

This book takes you step by step through the process of getting a grant. I want the book to be of significant value to you. This practical guide is based on my fifteen years of working with persons seeking grants. It contains the answers to their questions. We will look at everything you need to know to get the grant you want.

GRANT CHECKLIST

Preparation:

_____ Develop a well thought-out program to be funded.

_____ Get agreement to the program from relevant staff and administrators.

_____ Determine who will work on the grant. Assign responsibilities if more than one person will.

_____ Study the fundamentals of how to get a grant.

Finding a Funder:

_____ Locate and visit a library with a good grants collection. Ask a librarian to help you find what you need.

_____ Examine the reference resources which show funding sources. Start with the geographic and subject indexes, looking under several of the subject index terms.

_____ Focus first on local funding sources.

_____ Complete the funder identification work sheet to evaluate the potential funders by subject interests, geographic focus, size of grants, and types of support.

_____ Decide whether to seek foundation, corporate, or government funding.

_____ Choose a few likely funding sources based on the pattern of their past giving, and identify the best possibility.

_____ Contact the funder after your basic research to learn more about the funder.

_____ Know what specific information the funder wants you to send.

_____ Be aware of any proposal submission deadlines and final decision dates.

Writing the Grant Proposal:

_____ Review and follow all the instructions of the funder.

_____ Think about how long your proposal should be, and the format for it.

_____ Use the grant proposal work sheet to write a first draft, then elaborate in detail.

_____ Double-check the math in your budget.

_____ Edit the proposal and have someone inside and outside your organization do proofreading.

_____ Secure the signature of your C.E.O. or the president of your board on the letter proposal, or on the cover letter for the document proposal, and send the proposal.

Follow Up Actions:

_____ Follow up with the funding source about two weeks after mailing the proposal to see if they have any questions and to request an appointment.

_____ Find out why, if your grant proposal is rejected by a funder. Select the next funding source to approach.

_____ Make sure if you get a grant that you understand what the funder expects from you.

_____ Put on your calendar anything you must do to follow up.

_____ Establish financial and other record keeping systems.

_____ Send a thank you letter to the funder.

_____ Report to the funder on what the grant achieved.

Chapter 2

SOURCES OF GRANTS

**"I don't know what your destiny will be, but one thing I know.
The only ones among you who will be really happy
are those who have sought and found how to serve."
Albert Schweitzer**

Two cowboys were playing poker and drinking in an old west saloon one warm day. The liquor eventually began to take its toll. They drank up all their money and they had nothing left to bet with. So they began to make up poker bets in which the loser had to do something undesirable. The first cowboy lost and had to clean the dust off the boots of the other cowboy. Then the second cowboy lost. His friend grinned at him and asked, "Have you ever kissed a mule?" "No," said the other cowboy politely, "but I've always wanted to."

Perhaps you feel like that about seeking a grant.

The experience of getting a grant can be made fairly easy, and does not have to be perplexing. You can get a grant! You can get a grant! Among questions I'll answer for you are: Who makes grants? How do you find out about funding sources? How do you request grant funds?

Let me answer the first question now. Who makes grants? There are three main types of organizations that do: foundations, corporations, and government.

FOUNDATIONS

Foundations are a major source of grants. A foundation is a nonprofit organization which exists to serve the public good by making grants.

How many foundations would you guess there are in the United States? There are over 54,000 active foundations nationwide. So you have a wealth of options. Foundations awarded about $28 billion in grants last year. The largest twenty percent of foundations are responsible for giving ninety percent of the grant dollars. You can tell the money is concentrated at the top.

Foundations are required to give away a minimum of approximately five percent of their assets each year. The assets are stocks, bonds, and certificates of deposit. When the stock market goes up, the assets of most foundations go up, and they give away more money. Foundations are regulated by state and federal law. They file federal tax returns.

What kinds of foundations are there? There are big foundations such as the Gates Foundation, the Ford Foundation, and the Kellogg Foundation. They all have assets of over ten billion dollars. To come up with that kind of money Kellogg had to make a whole lot of little corn flakes. These big foundations have *a wide variety of subject interests*. They may donate nationwide. They each make hundreds of grants a year. Many of the grants are for hundreds of thousands of dollars and go to major projects of large national organizations. Competition for the grants is keen. The Rockefeller Foundation receives more than 12,000 grant requests a year. Of those, 75% are not considered because they are not appropriate requests. The boards of trustees of large national foundations are supported by the work of a professional staff. The staff, often the ones called "program officers," do most of the work involved in evaluating the grant requests, and they make recommendations about approving grants which are usually followed. As with most foundations, the board of trustees or a distribution committee of the board makes the final decisions about how much to grant and to whom.

There are medium size and small foundations. Often these will be family foundations in which the assets came from the donations of a wealthy family, which may still control the foundation. The foundations set policies on where they contribute, and for what. They each make dozens of grants a year. A foundation may give only in one city, or only for certain types of needs. If you call a foundation which is dedicated to helping the people of Lincoln County, for a grant in Madison County, the conversation will be… rather brief. How do you find out where and what a foundation wants to fund? **Research** will tell you that, and we will look at how to go about it. The smaller foundations do not have an office of their own, or any staff. They operate through the voluntary efforts of the trustees. A bank trust officer or an accountant may handle some of the financial matters.

Operating foundations are a special type of foundation. They operate their own charitable programs and usually exist to help one particular organization. A university, for instance, may have a foundation which helps support the university. This foundation aids only the university. Operating foundations will not be receptive to a grant request from you. Here again, research will tell you which foundations are best to approach or not approach.

Community foundations exist to meet the human needs in only one community. They often receive support from a wide range of donors in that community. Their subject interests are typically diverse, encompassing the artistic, educational, social, economic, health and recreational needs of a specific city or locality. The boards of trustees try to consider all local groups in making their grants. Community foundations are a focal point for community betterment.

> Each foundation is *unique*. A grant seeker should expect to see their variations. Like individuals, they each have different values, and different ways of doing things. Be flexible enough to adjust to their individual procedures. You should study potential funding sources and learn about them.

As with all types of donors, it may be possible to *develop relationships* with foundations. In fact, it is highly desirable to do so! You get to know them, they get to know you. You learn to like and trust them, they learn to like and trust you. When your next grant request comes in, they are favorably inclined toward you right from the start. Grants consultant Susan Golden says, "The most critical issues in a funding relationship are credibility and trust."

You can cultivate a positive relationship on an organizational, and a person to person level. Communicate with grant makers even when you don't need money. Put them on your mailing list. Send them on-going newsletters, press releases, or other information about your organization. You might even invite trustees or staff of the funding source for a tour of your organization, for lunch, to meet some of your trustees, or to events you host. Be responsive to funder concerns when working together. When you receive a grant, stay in touch about it and show the funder that your grant project has been successful.

There are several kinds of organizations that make grants other than the main three. These organizations make many, many fewer grants than foundations, corporations, or the government. Certain trusts make grants. From the point of view of a grant seeker, a trust operates much like a foundation. Treat a trust as if it were a foundation. Some associations, religious denominations, arts councils, and other groups also make grants. The basic principles in this book apply to getting grants from those sources.

CORPORATIONS

Corporations are another source of grants for you, in two ways. A corporation may have established a foundation to award grants. Also the corporation itself as a separate organization may award grants. So there are *two distinct possibilities*. Corporations and corporate foundations give away over $11 billion dollars a year for a great variety of needs. Large corporations generally give about $1,000 to $50,000 per grant. Locally based companies give amounts often corresponding to their net income. Except for big companies it is unrealistic to expect a grant of more than a few thousand dollars.

In addition to grants, foundations or corporations might give donations of a few hundred or a few thousand dollars to support a fund-raising event, or for annual support. You could also consider asking for an in-kind contribution of equipment, or even services. Perhaps the company would give you an old computer (two or three years old), or lend the services of an accountant, or a marketing expert.

A positive response to a request for a corporate grant will most often come from large companies headquartered in your local area. The next best options are large companies which have an office or a plant in your area, and after that companies with substantial sales in your area.

Companies which do not have a local office, but which are in a business relevant to what you do are possible funders. As an example, if you provide medical services, then medical product corporations might be considered. Some giant corporations think of themselves as corporate citizens of the nation, and they donate nationwide. However, because of that they are spread thin.

Generally you should consider foundations prior to companies in your search for a grant. Foundations exist to make grants, so they are much more focused on that than companies are.

A few corporations are concerned solely with assisting their own employees and employee families. Those corporations are not good prospects. Other corporations contribute only to the United Way because it is easier than setting up their own corporate system to donate to many different groups.

> Some corporate and foundation donors may give only to groups they
> "pre-select." They decide whom to contribute to, and they do not
> want to receive grant proposals. When a reference book says a
> funder gives only to pre-selected organizations, or says
> "applications not accepted," you should **skip over that funder**.

There are reference books which tell you about the giving policies of the largest companies in the country. While these companies are possibilities, don't be limited to just those huge national conglomerates. You can think of good sized local companies that are far better as possibilities, because they have a special interest in your community, which is their community. The executives and employees reside and work in your area. It is home to them. These local companies may have revenues of millions of dollars, may be capable of making substantial grants, and want to benefit the area where they are located.

Grant making is good public relations for companies. Businesses are always interested in being publicly recognized for helping a community.

Since local companies may not be mentioned in grant research materials, personal contacts often need to be made to gather information. You can call or write to companies that are not listed in reference books to find out whether their grant making policies are a good fit with your need. Personal contacts will be discussed in the next chapter.

It is not necessary to have a buddy at a foundation or corporation before you can obtain a grant. If someone on your board is a friend of someone on their board that may or may not help. The odds of having a connection like that where the relationship is more than just being acquaintances are not good. How likely is it that someone on your board will pipe up during a discussion of a corporation and say: "I know the chairman of the corporation trustees. He's my cousin, and boy does he owe me a big favor!" Sometimes making inside contacts will backfire. Staff or board members of the grant source may be offended by the attempted use of personal influence. Many grant distribution committees will not allow behind the scenes lobbying. If you want to use an inside contact, do so cautiously, testing the reactions before you proceed.

You might use creative methods of working with a company to meet your mutual needs. Here are some that have been successful. A museum sold a bank thousands of museum memberships which the bank gave as incentives to people who opened new accounts. A nonprofit musical group was paid by a corporation to stage a performance for its corporate employees and their families. A college showed a business how many of its graduates the business hires, leading the company to support the education of their future employees. A public television station received support from a manufacturer of children's products to air a children's program. Can you think of ways your organization can do things like these? Are there services you can provide to a business in exchange for a contribution?

GOVERNMENT

The third source of grants, the government, gives more grant money than any other source. In fact the federal government has several hundred grant programs. Available federal grants cover all kinds of needs: physical, educational, economic, etc., etc. Funding is available nationwide in almost all federal programs. The downside of federal grants is that the process can involve a lot of red tape and there may be many applicants for grants.

To find federal government grants, use the *Catalog of Federal Domestic Assistance*. It has an almost complete list of federal grant opportunities. Brand new programs and some smaller programs may not be mentioned. The *Catalog* is a valuable resource because you can find a wide variety of federal grant programs in one place. An "information contact" is listed so that you can ask a person your questions. You could ask for application advice, and about the level of competition for the grants.

With some federal programs, only state or local governments are eligible recipients. However those government units might then pass through the funds to nonprofit organizations. If the goals of a federal program are what you want to do, you should consult the information contact provided. Find out if a state or local government department may have received federal money, and see if they make grants to nonprofits. An example of local administration of federal money is the Community Development Block Grant Program.

There may be special councils or boards in your region that make grants. Examples would be a family services council, or a county alcohol and drug treatment board. Many of these organizations are affiliated with government. These quasi-governmental organizations get some government funds and have characteristics of both government and social service agencies. To locate the quasi-governmental organizations relevant to what you do, make phone calls to the United Way, city hall, the county commissioners, appropriate government departments, or social services agencies. You can then find out if any quasi-governmental organizations in your field make grants. Those organizations are seldom mentioned in grant research books.

> **State, county, and city government grants** are available. Each of those levels of government is a potential grant source. They run numerous grant making programs. The programs are designed to address many kinds of needs. Very few state or local governments print lists of the specific grants they offer. So finding out about the grant opportunities is a challenge. Because there are few published sources of information except on the federal level, person to person contacts are the way to proceed. For instance, you could call the mayor's office of your city to inquire about what kinds of grants the city makes. The different levels of government (possibly even townships) and their departments may have significant sums of money to distribute for the problems they choose to focus on.

In addition to grants, the government might also enter into a contract for your organization to provide goods or services. Government contracts to deliver social services of various kinds are widespread. To do business with the government you ought to make inquiries of an appropriate government department. Ask about what is available and what may be coming up.

The *most common mistakes* made by persons seeking government grants are: not calling the granting making department to gather information before sending in a grant request, not reading and following all the instructions, or not effectively presenting the grant seeking organization's abilities.

You hear a lot of talk about government programs being "cut back." Well, my experiences in Washington as a legislative assistant to a Congressman proved to me that the budget is seldom actually cut. When the federal plan was to spend five percent more, and Congress then spent only three percent more, there were screams about "slashing the budget." I have seen that type of situation happen many times. With the so-called, "current services budget" system used in Washington, the three percent increase was literally counted as a "cut." You and I might say, wait a minute... if the government spends more dollars than last year, it's really an increase. They don't think like that in Washington.

Some government programs have been reduced, but many more programs received substantial increases, resulting in large net increases in social welfare spending. The confusing federal budget system explains in part why you could hear about large budget cuts, while annual federal spending actually grew by over $500 billion during the last ten years. That was just the increase. Does that sound like slashing the budget to you? But I'm beginning to breath hard just thinking about it, so let me wrap this up. One day recently I looked at a federal budget summary, and counted 977 billion dollars (billion with a "b") spent yearly on social welfare needs by the federal government alone. That amount is about one-half of the total federal budget. The bottom line: there is government money available now, and there will be in the future.

We have now reviewed the basic kinds of funding sources. The following list shows **which sources are most likely to give you a grant**. The grant alternatives are in ranked order with number one as the best, number two as the next best, and on down the list.

1. Local foundations
2. Major corporations headquartered in your area
3. State and local government
4. Major corporations with employees or much of their sales in your area
5. Major foundations not located near your area
6. Federal government

Start with the grant sources at the top. Toward the bottom of this list, the chance of getting a grant goes below 50%. The list is valid for the average community oriented nonprofit seeking grants, however in your specific situation the best option for you may be different. The best one depends on your particular proposal and the individual funder. This list will give you an understanding of what you would learn from experience. Select an option that meets your need. I once heard of a young guy who wanted to leave home because he got tired of his mom telling him what to do. So he decided to join the Marines. In his case that was not the best option.

Federal grants are number six on the list. While money is available, most federal grants are very competitive. Some are not. A few federal grants go almost automatically to qualified recipients. Always inquire about whether there is a lot of competition for government grants. For instance, the federal information contact might tell you that 71 out of 83 proposals were funded in a government program in the last fiscal year. Those are favorable odds. But if only 9 out of 83 were funded, then you know how competitive this particular grant program is. The bad news is that the program is highly competitive. The good news is that you now know that, and you still have plenty of options. You might consider other government grants, a corporate grant, or a foundation grant.

Following this chapter there is a comparison of foundation funding and federal funding to help you better understand each. The table has a description in the column on the left side, and a contrasting description across from it on the right side. Corporate funding resembles foundation funding in this comparison. However, the research materials to use, and the average amounts given are different for corporations and foundations.

SPECIAL CONSIDERATIONS

In this next part we will cover a variety of questions and special considerations in getting grants. Why don't we start first with how you can set up a grant funding cycle.

Normally you should not approach a foundation or a corporation for a grant more often than every other year. Don't wear out your welcome. Most grant makers like to distribute money to a range of different organizations over time. If you have access to seven local funding sources with good potential, you could get grants from four in one year, and the other three sources the next year. That cycle could be repeated, with your nonprofit getting several grants a year for a long time to come.

> A tip, to get a lot of grants, send out a lot of *different* grant requests.
> The more times you try, the more successes you can have.

What about grants to individuals? It is not impossible, but foundations and corporations very seldom make a grant to an individual. They see their role as helping individuals through existing nonprofit groups. There are other options though. Government provides a multitude of direct and indirect assistance programs for individuals. For an individual's higher education needs, there are numerous books on government and non-government scholarships, grants, and loans. For research projects, there are special funding sources, such as those found in the *Annual Register of Grant Support* and the *Directory of Research Grants*. In addition note the comments below about working through a nonprofit. Researchers often work with nonprofits which are grant recipients.

It is not the purpose of this book to cover grants to individuals and businesses. However, a good size library will have helpful material about those kinds of grants. A book titled, *Foundation Grants to Individuals*, addresses some of the exceptions in which a foundation will make a grant to a person. Books are available that deal with the topic of obtaining funds for businesses. The *Catalog of Federal Domestic Assistance* lists assistance to persons in business or to those who want to start a business (under "Small Business" in the subject index).

Usually funders give grants *only* to nonprofits that have **501(c)(3)** status. That term, 501(c)(3), is used often in grants work. It refers to the section of the Internal Revenue Code which defines nonprofit organizations that are eligible for this tax exempt status. The 501(c)(3) organizations focus on social services, charitable activities, religion, health, arts, literary activities, science, or education. Most nonprofits are 501(c)(3) organizations. For more information about your tax exempt status check with your accountant or the I.R.S.

Governments are a special category. Governments (state, county, city, township, etc.) can obtain grants. The best of the options for a government seeking a grant is a grant from government. For instance, a city might seek a grant from the state government. Foundations and corporations might also make a grant to a government. Some foundations and corporations stay away from supporting government with grants because taxes already provide substantial public support.

Nonprofit agencies which are tax supported or related to government are often eligible to receive grants. These organizations may or may not be 501(c)(3)s. Public libraries, for example, are 501(c)(3)s.

Many foundations state up front in their printed materials that they give only to 501(c)(3) organizations. Educational institutions are an exception. Nonprofit schools can usually get grants regardless of their 501(c)(3) status. Individual funding sources, of course, ultimately decide who they actually will make grants to.

Profit making organizations almost never receive grants. The funds that may go to businesses are research grants, special government grants, or program related investments. A program related investment is a unique type of philanthropic funding that is not often available. Such an investment is made in a profit or nonprofit organization to achieve a funder's community service goals. For example, a foundation may loan or invest (not give) part of its assets to an organization that deliberately hires many persons formerly getting public welfare assistance. The assets are invested where they will achieve a charitable purpose.

Let me mention here that sometime you may receive or become aware of a grant maker's request for proposals, an **RFP**. The grant maker is requesting that proposals be developed to deal with a specified need. The grant maker will then fund one or more of the proposals submitted. You are free to choose if you want to respond to an RFP with a proposal to tackle the problem using the grant.

Perhaps you have not yet formed a nonprofit, but you have a project in mind which requires grant funding. To get a grant you could form the organization and incorporate, then get the organization approved by the I.R.S. Tax Exempt Organizations Division, and your state. It takes a few months. A fine introduction to this topic is *Starting and Running a Nonprofit Organization* by Joan Hummel.

Sometimes brand new nonprofits have unrealistic expectations about getting sizable grants. Without a record of success it is difficult to obtain a grant of $50,000 or $100,000.

A recent college graduate went for a job interview. The interview went smoothly, and the topic of money came up. The interviewer asked how much salary the young man expected. The graduate spoke up, "Well, I think about $80,000 a year to start would be acceptable, if the benefit package is solid." The interviewer replied, "We could offer you that with full health coverage, generous stock options, an outstanding retirement plan, and as a company car, a new red BMW." "Wow!" exclaimed the young man, "You're kidding." The interviewer replied, "Yes. But you started it." (It is wise to be realistic.)

One option for individuals or new organizations is to work through an already recognized 501(c)(3) nonprofit. Select an organization with which you want to cooperate, and ask them to act as your "fiscal agent." They would be the recipient of the grant money, but then pass it on to you to carry out the grant program. The fiscal agent must have final authority over the use of the grant funds. You could work in partnership with them to achieve mutually agreed upon goals. You would negotiate with them on the details of how the grant would be spent, and how much support you are to receive. That agreement would be reflected in the grant proposal you prepare together. The fiscal agent is legally obligated to spend the grant money in the way the proposal states.

THE SHOTGUN METHOD

Once you have written a proposal it is not a good idea to flood the mail with it. Approach each potential funder on a one by one basis. It is inappropriate to ask for the very same grant money from many sources simultaneously. That is called "the shotgun method" of trying to get a grant. Instead, ask one source at a time. Know enough about the funder you request a grant from so that you have a good chance of getting the grant. You should send a proposal to grant makers sequentially, not simultaneously. That is proper form and is expected. In addition that avoids the loss of credibility from returning one grant if you get two identical checks. A funder whose check is returned will be much less inclined to take your next grant request seriously.

If you do need more than one grant, for a very expensive project, **let each grant maker know what other grant makers you are also contacting**. In that way you are being up front about what you are doing, and you avoid a problem. Grant makers talk among themselves, and they won't like it if they find you are keeping them in the dark.

Say you employ the shotgun method and mail identical $35,000 grant requests to four foundations, without letting them know about each other. The executive director of one of the foundations eventually hears that you will receive a grant from another foundation. He might be tempted to think something like this: "I spent a lot of time studying your request, our board of trustees did too. We had already set aside money to fund your proposal, and turned down other nonprofits so we could fund yours. What you did creates problems for us. Why didn't you tell us what you were doing?" If a person came to your organization to ask for specific assistance, but then went to two other organizations for duplicate assistance, you might be annoyed. There would be wasted effort and confusion. You don't want to offend grant makers because they may not consider funding you in the future. If that happens very often, your range of options may dry up.

If you need $120,000 you could ask three foundations to each give $40,000. That is a standard way of building up a large sum. It is much easier to get one funder to pay the whole amount, but using multiple funders is sometimes the only realistic possibility. When you explain what you are doing there is no problem. You should name the foundations in the proposal cover letter. You are not in this case asking them all for the very same thing, the final total of $120,000. Each foundation has a part to play and receives a sincere request. Keep each grant maker informed of your progress in getting grants.

When there are several funders who are asked for exactly the same grant, they might think that another funder will make the grant, so their organization does not need to. If all the funders think that, there is trouble. It will slow down the process of getting a grant to go to one grant source at a time, but that is the way it should be done. In your situation you may not be able to wait several months, only to be turned down by the one funder you contacted. You may choose to submit the proposal to several funders simultaneously. However, let me say again, be sure to indicate you are approaching other funders also, so that all those involved know what the situation is.

SELECTING THE RIGHT FUNDING SOURCE

We have examined the three general types of funding sources. This section will help you select the specific one which will make a grant to your organization.

What should you look at in seeking the funder most likely to award your organization a grant? **Past giving is a key point**. You should look for the pattern of a funder's past giving to determine what it will do in the future. If a foundation has contributed to a program like yours in the past, it may well do so again.

> You want to find *a funding source whose interests match your own.*
> When your goal is one of their goals, then you have found a partner.
> You provide the ability and the plan, they provide the dollars. The
> funder wants you to be successful in achieving your mutual goals.
> Your success is their success.

You do research to find a funder with a proven interest in a project like yours. As you consider funders, try to compile a list of a few possibilities. That way you have alternatives ready. If the first one does not work out, you don't have to start the research again. You just go to the next funder on your prospect list. Save the list for future use in seeking other related grants.

By making good choices about grant makers you save yourself much time. Rather than having to approach a funder and waiting for a response, only to be turned down, you go first to a funder which will make a grant to you. Accept the situation if a funder's past giving indicates no interest in your funding need. If one funder is not right for your organization, the funder won't change, but you can simply select another funder.

Research in the reference sources described in the next chapter will give you the facts you need to make good choices. Also, some grant makers have printed materials that will indicate their giving interests and procedures.

The four main criteria to consider in selecting a funder are: subject interests, geographic focus, size of grants, and types of support. You need to identify a funder that makes grants for your subject, *and* in your location, *and* in the amount you want, *and* for the type of support you want.

Subject Interests

You can learn what the subject interests of a funder are. What problems or needs does the funder focus its attention on? What organizations and groups of people does the funder assist? Has the funder made grants for social services, health, education, or poverty related programs? All of these? Any of these? Has it *ever* funded a program in your subject interest in the past? Has it *never* funded a program in your subject interest in the past?

The grant reference books list the funder's subject interests. In addition, you can draw your own conclusions by knowing about past grants. If a corporation has made a grant to an agency for distribution of health information in your city, this suggests the corporation might make a grant to another agency for health services there. In looking for *a precedent*, if you can find a past grant for a subject similar to yours, that is usually good enough to demonstrate the funder's interest. Don't interpret past giving too narrowly. For example, if a grant maker has contributed to construct a baseball field in a public park, this suggests a concern about youth, recreation, and community development, not just athletics.

> When a funding source has shown an interest in many subjects, you can correctly draw the conclusion that it is *not specialized*. Therefore, the door is open to you whatever your interest. Foundations that donate for many kinds of needs are called **"general purpose foundations**.**"** Some other foundations are, by contrast, interested in only one or a very few subjects. Knowing which are the general purpose foundations in your area is very useful.

Usually community foundations are general purpose foundations. They want to address *whatever needs exist* in their communities. Whatever idea you have for a grant, a general purpose foundation will consider it.

To be realistic, the grant resource books are not absolutely complete lists of all the subjects foundations and corporations might support. The subjects listed are ones of proven interest. Perhaps you have a good reason to believe a funder might support your grant plan, even though a reference book does not show that funder has an interest in your subject. To be sure, check another grant information resource, or contact the grant maker directly.

Related to what is funded are the **limitations** which exist, what is not funded. For instance, a large majority of funders do not make grants to religious groups for religious purposes. Religious organizations, though, have many other fundraising options available, such as support from members, planned giving, or capital campaigns. (We will review the options at the end of this book.) If a religious organization has a program which has a secular purpose, then a grant for that program is treated like a grant for any other nonprofit organization. Many churches and synagogues have programs which meet society's needs: they feed the hungry, perform social services, support recovery groups, and so forth. When seeking grants for social service initiatives, a church is on the same footing as other community organizations.

There are some foundations which do provide grants for religious purposes. In fact, certain foundations specialize in religion. Foundations supporting religion can be found in the grant resource books we will consider. In addition there are directories which focus on the bigger foundations which make religious grants. Two of these directories are the *National Guide to Funding in Religion* and *Fund Raiser's Guide to Religious Philanthropy*.

Sometimes you will find in a list of grants that a church received a grant. This may mean a board member or the person who set up the foundation is affiliated with that church. You should be aware that the grant maker may not have an interest in other churches.

Certain religious denominations have their own programs for making grants. They are potential grant sources for religious and non-religious organizations.

Geographic Focus

Does the funding organization award grants in only one locality, or nationwide? Where has the grant money usually gone? Any to your area? None to your area? Reference books will describe the geographic focus of the grant maker. It was mentioned earlier that this point is a decisive one. Often funders give only to certain locations. You will see in doing research that geographic limitations are very common. Look for funders which are in the locality that will benefit from the grant.

You are more likely to get a grant for a project in your community from a foundation close to your community than from a foundation in another region. It stands to reason that a foundation is most interested in its own community. Because you generally have substantially **better odds with local funding sources**, give consideration to funders from your city or county first. Then consider funders from your part of the state.

The best options will usually be within about 30 miles of your nonprofit. If you are located in a rural area, you may have to consider more than just a 30 mile radius to find appropriate funders.

I am not saying you cannot get a grant from a funding source located in another state. You might. Local funders are good possibilities, but they are not your only possibilities. The organizations which are most likely to get a grant from an out of state funder are large institutions.

Size of Grants

Does the prospective grant source make *grants in the amount you need*? What is the dollar range of the grants distributed? How much are the average grants? If a donor does not contribute as much as you want, then you are put in the position of bypassing that donor, or using more than one source of funds.

As noted earlier, even small corporations and foundations typically distribute their grants to a dozen or more recipients. Larger funders make many more grants than that. If a corporation gives a total of $200,000 a year in grants, it is unlikely to make one grant to your organization for $90,000. The average amount distributed will be much lower.

If you ask for too much you may hurt your chance of getting the grant. When you ask for an amount above the high end of the average range you may be asking for trouble. If the grants are almost all between $5,000 and $25,000 you might reasonable ask for up to $25,000.

A small foundation may give grants for projects exactly like yours, so it is not to be ignored. However, other things being equal, you are generally better off approaching larger grant makers. They simply have more money. The bank robber Willie Sutton was once asked, "Why do you rob banks?" He replied, "Because that's where the money is." You should go to the bigger funding sources for the same reason, because that's where the money is. One technique of funder research is to start by checking the ten largest foundations in your vicinity to see if they are good prospects.

Types of Support

Grant makers often have policies on the types of support they provide. Does a grant maker provide support for **seed money** to start new organizations? For **building funds**? For **operating support**? You should determine whether your need coincides with what a grant maker offers. It may be that a grant maker contributes to your subject interest, but not for the particular kind of support you have in mind. For instance, if you want a grant to build an **endowment**, or to erase your organizational **budget deficit**, some funders will not contribute for those types of expenses. Almost all funders provide support for new programs and services, sometimes called **program development**. If you want that type, you are well positioned.

Type of support is a general category and may also be called nature of support. Some specific types of support are in bold above. Among other types of support are: **capital campaigns, continuing support, emergency funds, equipment, loans, matching funds**, and **research**. Which type of support do you want?

A given corporation might specify in their guidelines that they make grants for equipment, but not for research. That is good to know if you are looking for a grant to purchase equipment. That is also good to know if you are looking for a grant to do a research study, because at least you won't waste your time approaching that particular corporation.

Many grant makers prefer to support new initiatives rather than to provide operating support. Operating support is mixed into your organization's annual budget. Operating support is not for any specific purpose. Even if a grant is not for operating support, it can still help your overall budget. A grant to fund a new program you would otherwise have to pay for takes pressure off your budget. The grant frees up money that can be used for other budget expenses.

In the *Catalog of Federal Domestic Assistance* there are 15 types of assistance. Project grants are the type that will most often benefit a nonprofit. The types of assistance are listed and defined in the front of the *Catalog*.

Type of support is usually the most difficult of the four criteria to pin down. Reference books may not completely list all the types of support a funder will supply. Do not conclude that because you can't find the type of support you want listed in a reference book entry about a funder that you cannot get that type of support. If your type of support is listed, you are set. If it is not listed, check further. When you are in doubt about a type of support, consult the funder. Sometimes you might choose to proceed without a solid understanding about a type of support a funder provides. For each of the other three basic criteria, however, you really should know that there is a match with the funding source.

Deadlines are sometimes a factor to consider. There may be two funders who are serious possibilities, but one makes grants next month, while the other makes grants six months from now. That could determine which one better suits your need. So knowing about deadlines and when grant checks will be mailed out is valuable.

Use the funder identification work sheet on page 27 as a way to evaluate potential funders. Make as many copies as you need, using one for each grant source. This work sheet is designed to assist you in the funder selection process and give you practical guidance on the issues to consider. In doing research you can rule out some funders and add others to your prospect list. Then choose the best possibility.

We have considered funding options, and how to select one. In the next chapter we will look at the resources which provide the information you need to make the selection. The resources will help you identify the grant maker which is best for your organization.

Foundations

There are many foundations, and thus a diverse variety of subject interests. You can ask foundations to support a project you design to meet your goals.

Two basic reference sources for foundation grants are: *The Foundation Directory* and *The Foundation Directory Part 2.*

Foundations often do not have a special application format. If not, you could use the eight part proposal style (in this book) to write your grant request.

Usually a grant ranges from $1,000 to $100,000, and is a one-time grant.

The grant process varies somewhat from one foundation to another. Each sets its own policies and procedures.

Decisions are made by the board of trustees of the foundation, who typically volunteer their service. Some larger foundations have a professional staff.

Federal Government

Federal government interests are limited to the problems that have been selected for government focus. Your grant program must fit their goals.

Two basic reference sources for federal grants are: the *Catalog of Federal Domestic Assistance* and the *Federal Register.*

The federal government often uses Standard Form 424, plus special forms they designate. The eight part proposal style can be used when there is no other specified format.

A grant may be tens to hundreds of thousands of dollars, and be on-going year after year.

The grant process varies among departments and is bureaucratic. There are legal regulations involved and strings attached.

Program officers administer federal grant programs and the selection of grant recipients. Grant officers administer grant funds.

FUNDER IDENTIFICATION WORK SHEET

(Make as many copies as necessary, using one per funder.
Be sure to record the dates and content of contacts with a funder.)

Funder name:

Address:

Phone number:

Contact person and title:

Sources and dates of this information:

Annual giving (total amount and average grant size):

Does this grant source have subject interests that match ours?

Do they give in our geographic area?

Do they give in the amount we need?

Do they give for the type of support we need?

What are the limitations on their giving?

Does the funder have any deadlines?

Does the funder publish an annual report, giving guidelines, or an application form?

Which type of initial approach and grant proposal does the funder prefer?

What information does the funder request in a proposal?

Are there any special considerations about this funder of which we should be aware?

What contact have we had in the past with this funder?

On a one to ten scale, with ten as the best, how does this funder rate as a grant prospect?

What questions do we have for the funder?

Chapter 3

FINDING THE INFORMATION YOU NEED

**"...let us run with perseverance
the race that is set before us...."
The Bible, Hebrews 12:1**

One director of a foundation, Martin Teitel, has stated that his foundation receives, "dozens of proposals from organizations that clearly never did a lick of homework...." He said he knows there was no research done because the organizations are sending very inappropriate requests asking for kinds of grants his foundation clearly does not fund. Mr. Teitel said of the persons mailing the misdirected proposals, "I often wonder if these same people try to buy their groceries in the hardware store." Well, perhaps Mr. Teitel woke up feeling a bit crabby that morning, but you can see his point.

Funders get many inappropriate grant proposals. In a recent survey of foundation administrators, the most frequent suggestion they offered grant seekers was: **learn about the foundation to be approached**. This includes reading foundation application guidelines carefully, and doing research to understand what the foundation is willing to finance. One expert, Andy Robinson, has said about approaching funders, "Don't knock on the door until you know who is inside." This short statement summarizes a key principle about interacting with grant makers.

You *dramatically increase your chance of getting a grant* when you apply to a funder that is seriously interested in what you want to do. This chapter will help you with the know-how. You can then move into action and start looking at specific funding sources.

Here is a riddle I have heard. Three children were sitting on a sofa watching television. Two of them decided they should get up and do their homework. How many children were left watching television? Three, because deciding to do something and doing it are not the same. Can you see how that might apply to doing research?

You don't have to bring a tent, sleeping bag, and backpack to the library in doing your research, but you should spend some time with the research materials. The more you know, the more likely you are to get a grant. Knowledge really is power. In obtaining a grant, as with many other endeavors, the best helping hand a person can find is at the end of one of his arms.

To approach a grant maker without doing research is gambling and hoping to get lucky. If you want to try your luck, then buying lottery tickets is an easier option, though we will not be going into the finer points of that particular fund-raising methodology.

Basically, I want to answer two questions about the research materials. How do you find what you need in them? What information do the research materials contain?

To answer the first question now, the answer is the same for all the books. To find useful information, check in the indexes. Many of the books have more than one index in the back of the book. For instance, in *The Foundation Directory* there are indexes for: subject, geographic location, personal name (of a donor, trustee, or officer), type of support, new grant makers, and foundation name.

> You can *use the indexes as the starting points in your search*. If you want to find the foundations in your area, check the geographic index. If you want to find who is funding education grants, check the subject index under "Education" and related terms, such as "Higher education." **The more terms you check, the more information you find**. Therefore, always check several subject terms.

If you look in *The Foundation Directory* subject index under "Handicapped" you will find... nothing. That is because the publisher uses the term "Disabled" instead. It is highly important to use the words they use. *The Foundation Directory* has a list of terms used in the subject index, at the front of that index. The list will help you select the right subject terms to check. Otherwise you could be looking under the wrong words and find little or nothing, when there is actually much to be found. Other books often have similar lists of terms used.

Subject interests and geographic interests of a funder are a couple of the key factors to consider as you begin. They should be found together, you want to find your subject, funded in your area. Some books may use the headings "Purpose and activities" or "Fields of interest" to describe subject areas funded. *The Foundation Directory* has listings in the subject index that indicate the foundations making grants for a particular subject by state, for example, community development in Florida. Read the information containing entries in the main section of the directory for each of the listed foundations. Also consider the other previously described factors in making a good match: size of grants, and types of support. In this way you find the most appropriate funders.

Another approach is to begin the grant search by making a list of foundations and corporations in your geographic area, then checking them to see what they fund. You always begin with the index. In this method you start with the location, in the other you start with the subject. As mentioned before, local funders are *more likely* to make a grant to you than other funders, but local funders are not your only possibilities. If you live in a metropolitan area with dozens of sizable foundations, then starting with the subject approach is faster. You should check both the location and subject indexes before you finish the research, if you want to find a number of funding sources.

The sources of information listed below will be discussed in this chapter. If you can remember just the first two sources, you will be off to a good start. If you can remember all these sources, then you are doing very well. And if you can't remember any, well... getting a grant is like an open book test. You can always look up the answers as you need them.

Key Information Sources:
➢ *The Foundation Directory*
➢ *The Foundation Directory Part 2*
➢ *Catalog of Federal Domestic Assistance*
➢ 990-PFs
➢ Personal Contacts

(On the next page is an example of the geographic index in The Foundation Directory. To completely read this example is unnecessary. Look it over for a minute to get an idea of what it contains.)

FOUNDATION DIRECTORY GEOGRAPHIC INDEX

Foundations in boldface type make grants on a national, regional, or international basis; the others generally limit giving to the city or state in which they are located. For local funders with a history of giving in another state, consult the "see also" references at the end of each state section.

ALABAMA

Alexander City: Russell 70
Andalusia: Dixon 35
Anniston: Stringfellow 80, **Zeiger 91**
Atmore: **Corman 30**
Baileyton: Walker 86
Birmingham: Abroms 1, Alabama 2, **Altec 4,** Barber 7,
    Bashinsky 8, Bolden 12, Brock 13, Bruno 14, Bruno
    15, Bruno 16, Caring 17, Carson 18, Citation 22,
    Cobb 24, Cohron 25, Community 27, Compass 29,
    Daniel 32, Dixon 34, **Fig 37,** Griffin 41, Hackney
    42, Harrison 43, Healthsouth 44, Hess 46, Hess 47,
    JJE 49, Johnson 50, Kaul 51, Lakeshore 53, Linn 54,
    Mayer 59, McWane 63, Meyer 65, **Ruttenberg 71,**
    Scrushy 72, Shook 73, Sonat 77, Stephens 78,
    Stockham 79, To 82, Unus 84, **Vulcan 85,** Webb 88,
    Whatley 89, Williamson 90
Brewton: McMillan 62
Camden: Wallace 87
Childersburg: Christian 21
Decatur: Baker 6
Dothan: Dove 36, McLendon 61
Enterprise: Gibson 39
Fairhope: **Coastal 23**
Gulf Shores: Meyer 64
Guntersville: Glassco 40
Madison: Alpha 3
Mobile: Bedsole 9, Community 28, Crampton 31,
    DeBakey 33, Florence 38, Hearin 45, Laidlaw 52,
    May 58, Mitchell 66, Smith 75, Treadwell 83

Montgomery: Aronov 5, Blount 11, Central 19, Loeb
     55, Lowder 56, Lowder 57, McKinney 60, **Randa
     69,** Simpson 74, Smith 76
Mountain Brook: Hill 48
Selma: Talton 81
Sylacauga: Comer 26
Tallassee: Blount 10
Tuscaloosa: Moody 67, Phifer 68
Valley: Charter 20

see also 1789, 1907, 2250, 2265, 2282, 2316, 2428,
     2456, 2487, 2832, 3160, 3206, 4616, 4916, 4951,
     5952, 7558, 9157, 10267, 10314

ALASKA

Anchorage: Alaska 92, Atwood 94, Carr 95, **CIRI 96,**
     Nolan 98, Rasmuson 99
Barrow: Arctic 93
Fairbanks: Doyon 97

see also 225, 839, 945, 1344, 1395, 7447, 8359, 8426,
     10043, 10058, 10059, 10060, 10074, 10076, 10112,
     10118, 10136, 10158, 10197

ARIZONA

Flagstaff: BF 106
Mesa: **Davis 110**
Paradise Valley: Peck 134
Phoenix: A.P.S. 100, **AGCS 103,** Arizona 104, Aurora
     105, Burns 107, Dorrance 112, Dougherty 113,
     Farrington 116, Flinn 117, Grossman 119, Levine
     123, Lincoln 124, Long 125, Louis 126, Marley
     128, Osborne 132, Pendleton 135, Phelps 136,
     Solheim 143, Steele 148, Viad 154, Wharton 156,
     Whiteman 157
Prescott: **Kieckhefer 122,** Morris 131

Scottsdale: **Agape 102,** Cummings 109, du Bois 115,
    Globe 118, Herberger 120, Marshall 130, Reese
    137, **Schumann 141,** Schupak 142, Stardust 147
Sun Lakes: Robson 139
Tempe: Tell 151
Tucson: Absolon 101, Community 108, DeGrazia 111,
    Dove 114, Hermundslie 121, M.A.R.K. 127,
    Marshall 129, **Research 138,** Schmidt 140,
    Southern 144, **Southwestern 145,** Spalding 146,
    Strauss 149, Tankersley 150, Tucson 152, **Van
    Schaick 153**
Wickenburg: Webb 155
Yuma: **Pasquinelli 133**

_____

see also 235, 509, 781, 869, 1180, 2045, 2521, 2584,
    2798, 2840, 3050, 3183, 3435, 3996, 4056, 4690,
    4775, 4956, 5172, 5321, 5956, 6218, 6268, 6513,
    6722, 7456, 8163, 8348, 8550, 9274, 9368, 9877,
    10056, 10197, 10370, 10480

ARKANSAS

Arkadelphia: Ross 179, Sturgis 183
Bentonville: McKinney 171, Wal 188, Walton 190
De Queen: De Queen 161
De Witt: Ferguson 162
El Dorado: Merkle 172, Murphy 173, Union 187
Little Rock: Altheimer 158, Arkansas 159, Bodenhamer
    160, **Frueauff 164,** Hussman 166, McAdams 170,
    Ottenheimer 174, Regions 175, Riggs 176,
    Rockefeller 177, Rockefeller 178, Smith 181, **Taylor
    184,** Wrape 192
Malvern: Sturgis 182
Newport: Frankum 163
Pine Bluff: Trinity 185
Siloam Springs: **Windgate 191**
Springdale: Jones 167, Jones 168, Jones 169,
    Schmieding 180, **Tyson 186,** Walker 189
Van Buren: Hamm 165

_____

Essentially you will be going through just three main steps. Check the indexes. Read about the funder. Evaluate the funder using the criteria mentioned previously.

If you really think of research as optional in securing a grant, consider the comments of these two experienced foundation executives. People in the grants field know how vital research is to success. To learn some of the basics about a funding source just makes sense.

"Find out as much as you can about the foundation. Target your approach- the rifle rather than the shotgun approach." (Ilene Mack)

"Be thorough in your preparation and research before attempting to initiate contact with a funder." (Charles Johnson)

As we review the major reference resources, write down the names of the ones you want to consult and take your notes with you to the library. Or, make notes in this book and take it with you. You do not need to examine all the resources listed in this chapter. I will make recommendations. Think of this chapter as a menu. Choose the resources that will be of most value in your individual situation.

Larger libraries have many of the materials discussed here. Ask a librarian for help in finding what is needed. Copy the few reference book pages of most relevance to you so that you can keep them for future use.

For best results consider more than one year's information. If you look at two foundation tax returns, each covering a different year, you will have a broader perspective on what a funder has given. Or, you could study a foundation in the latest two annual volumes of *The Foundation Directory*.

The research sources are not perfect. The sources occasionally have errors, or are sometimes based on information a few years old. However, we must use what is available for grant seekers.

The following research sources (except as noted) will show for each funder: address, phone number, contact person, financial data, subject interests, types of support, limitations on giving (often geographic), and application guidance. Sometimes deadlines are included.

Start with the first two books. They cover 95% of all foundation giving. Only the small foundations are not included in them. **You may be able to find a foundation funder from this set alone.**

BOOKS

The Foundation Directory: This annual book has data on about 10,000 of the largest American foundations. This is a nice book to use because it has a significant amount of information about each listed foundation and is well indexed. The book covers about 20% of foundations. Those are the biggest ones, and they give a substantial majority of the money granted. Names of trustees, number of staff, and sometimes a list of the foundation's bigger grants are displayed. There is a supplement to the directory midway through the year.

The Foundation Directory Part 2: This directory includes about 10,000 middle size foundations. Part 2 picks up where the book above leaves off. The format is the same as *The Foundation Directory*.

The Foundation 1,000: The 1,000 wealthiest foundations in the nation are shown in this research tool. Each foundation entry is long and quite thorough. Five indexes including a subject and a geographic index are supplied. There is tremendous competition for grants from these foundations. Only if your nonprofit is located close to one of these foundations, or if you have a grant project of major significance should you consider these foundations.

National Directory of Corporate Giving: Approximately 3,000 large corporate grant makers are described here. There is the same kind of basic information found in *The Foundation Directory*. Sometimes a brief list of sample grants is shown. Indexes include subject, geographic focus, and type of business.

Catalog of Federal Domestic Assistance: This government publication is a compendium of over 1,400 federal programs, of which several hundred are grant programs. Each entry has great detail. The *Catalog* shows who is eligible for a specific grant: states, local governments, or nonprofits. Related programs which might be relevant to your nonprofit are also mentioned in the program description, and you should consider them. There are several indexes. Start with the subject index. The *Catalog* is available in a variety of formats: loose leaf binder pages, CD-ROM, the Internet, and disks.

Federal Register: As a Monday through Friday daily periodical, among many other functions, it presents the newest federal government grant opportunities. The grant opportunities are usually listed as notices in the contents index at the front of each volume. The index is arranged by federal department. Details about the grants are given later in the periodical. There are also monthly and annual indexes. To use this periodical effectively requires a consistent commitment of time to review the *Federal Register* regularly. Most grant seekers will consider this resource optional.

The Foundation Center headquartered in New York City publishes the first four books in the preceding resource list. The Foundation Center is devoted to advancing knowledge about foundations and grants.

Cooperating Collections

Working with the Foundation Center are a network of libraries across the nation, called "cooperating collections." Those libraries collaborate with the Foundation Center to supply grant information. The cooperating collections have all the main grant resources and usually have more information about foundations and grants than other libraries.

There will be a librarian at the cooperating collection who is knowledgeable about grant research. **The cooperating collection libraries can be located by calling the Foundation Center at: 1 (800) 424-9836.** The cooperating collection library use is free, and they usually host grant workshops too.

You can call a library to find out whether they have the books you want. Don't try to do research at a small library that does not have the basic books. You will benefit from using good resources.

If you want to start your research at a library close to your home, find a library that at least has *The Foundation Directory*, *The Foundation Directory Part 2*, and the *Catalog of Federal Domestic Assistance*. If a library does not have all three of those, call a larger library to ask if they do. Don't defeat yourself by trying to obtain a grant without using the proper tools.

On pages that follow there are samples of typical information contained in *The Foundation Directory* and the *Catalog of Federal Domestic Assistance*. (In the *Catalog of Federal Domestic Assistance* when you see the abbreviation "CFR" that stands for *Code of Federal Regulations*, which is a large technical set of federal rules. The CFR provides background about the administration and procedures of grant programs.)

FOUNDATION DIRECTORY INDEX

In the **subject index** under "Children & youth, services" the Ayrshire Foundation is shown in the California section. A person looking for a grant for services to children and youth in California could turn to entry number 236 and examine the Ayrshire Foundation as a potential funder. The information about this foundation shows they made some grants for children, which is why they are listed under that subject in the index.

Children & youth, services

California: Alliance 195, **American 205,** Arata 213,
     Argyros 218, AT&T 225, **Atkinson 226,** Autry 231,
     Ayrshire 236, **Azus 237, Baker 240,** Bandai 243,

FOUNDATION DIRECTORY

As you look at Foundation Directory information, especially note the following:

Assets
Range in grant size
Purpose and activities
Fields of interest
Types of support
Limitations on giving
Application information
Past grants (a partial list)

All the items above are in the entry for the Ayrshire Foundation. Can you find them?

236

The Ayrshire Foundation
301 E. Colorado Blvd., No. 802
Pasadena, CA 91101   (602) 795-7583
Contact: James N. Gamble, Pres.

Established in 1998 in CA.
Donor(s): James N. Gamble
Foundation type: Independent
Financial data: (yr. Ended 05/31/01): Assets,
$14, 029,177 (M); expenditures $788,763;
qualifying distributions, $767,772; giving
activities include $773,825 for 18 grants (high:
$160,000; low: $6,000).
Purpose and activities: Giving primarily for
education and a seminar center; some giving
also for youth services, arts and recreation.
Fields of interest: Museums; arts/cultural
programs; education; recreation, centers;
children & youth, services; aging, centers &
services.
Types of support: Capital campaigns;
building/renovation; equipment; land
acquisition; endowments; program
development; conferences/seminars;
professorships; scholarship funds;
matching/challenge support.
Limitations: Giving primarily in CA.
Application information: Preference given to
communities where one or more trustees
maintain domiciles. Application form not
required.
  Initial approach: Letter
  Deadline(s): None
  Board meeting date(s): Apr. and Oct.

Officers and Directors: * James N. Gamble,*
Pres.; Margaret G. Boyer,* V.P.; Tracy G. Hirrel,*
V.P.; Susan T. House, Secy.; Thomas S. Jones,
Treas.; Peter S. Boyer, Helen Lee Gamble,
Richard J. Hirrel.
Number of staff: None
EIN: 954690418
Selected grants: The following grants were
reported in 2000.
$80,000 to Pasadena Senior Center, Pasadena,
    CA. For endowment for training program.
$65,164 to Union Station Foundation,
    Pasadena, CA. For building and endowment
    campaign.
$60,000 to California Academy of Sciences, San
    Francisco, CA. For teaching exhibition.
$52,200 to Hillsides Home for Children,
    Pasadena, CA. For mental health program.
$50,000 to University of Michigan, Ann Arbor,
    MI. For faculty endowment.
$30,000 to Randall Museum, San Francisco,
    CA. For recycling exhibit.
$25,000 to Rose Bowl Aquatics Center,
    Pasadena, CA. Toward a new pool.
$25,000 to Young and Healthy, Pasadena, CA.
    For health insurance for indigent children.
$17,000 to Huntington Library, Art Collections
    and Botanical Gardens, San Marino, CA. For
    Botanical Teaching Center.
$10,000 to Southern Exposure Gallery, San
    Francisco, CA. For summer artist program.

CATALOG OF FEDERAL DOMESTIC ASSISTANCE INDEX

Looking in the **subject index** under "Volunteers" there is a listing for the Retired Senior Volunteer Program, 94.002. Turning to that entry number, a person will find the program description.

Volunteers
childhood immunization 93.268
Foster Grandparent Program (FOP) 94.011
management expertise 59.026
offices of volunteer services 94.011
Retired Senior Volunteer Program (RSVP) 94.002
Service Corps of Retired Executives Association (SCORE) 59.026
tax counseling, elderly 21.006
VISTA 94.013
women 17.700
Women's Bureau 17.700

CATALOG OF FEDERAL DOMESTIC ASSISTANCE

Note these important sections of the federal program description:

Objectives
Types of Assistance
Eligibility Requirements
Application and Award Process
Financial Information
Information Contact
Related Programs

All the items above are in the entry for the Retired Senior Volunteer Program. Can you find them? (You do not need to read this lengthy program description. You can get an understanding of the contents by looking just at the headings.)

94.002 RETIRED AND SENIOR VOLUNTEER PROGRAM (RSVP)

FEDERAL AGENCY: CORPORATION FOR NATIONAL AND COMMUNITY SERVICE.

AUTHORIZATION: Domestic Volunteer Service Act of 1973, as amended, Title II, Part A, Section 201, Public Law 93-113, 42 U.S.C. 5001, as amended; National and Community Service Trust Act of 1993, Public Law 103-82.

OBJECTIVES: To provide a variety of opportunities for retired persons, age 55 or older, to serve their community through significant volunteer service.

TYPES OF ASSISTANCE: Project Grants.

USES AND USE RESTRICTIONS: Volunteers are not to supplant hiring, displace employed workers, or impair existing contracts for service. No agency supervising volunteers shall request or receive compensation for services of the volunteers. Volunteers are not to be involved in and funds are not to be used for religious activities, labor or anti-labor organizations, lobbying, or partisan or non-partisan political activities. Grants may be used for staff salaries and fringe benefits, staff travel, equipment, and related expenses, and for volunteer out-of-pocket expenses, primarily for transportation. An amount equal to 25 percent of the Federal share must be used for direct volunteer expenses. In addition, eligible agencies or organizations may, under a Memorandum of Agreement with the Corporation for National Service, receive technical assistance and materials to aid in establishing and operating non-Corporation funded RSVP projects using local funds.

ELIGIBILITY REQUIREMENTS:

  Applicant Eligibility: Grants are made only to State and local government agencies and private nonprofit organizations.

  Beneficiary Eligibility: Persons age 55 and older who are willing to volunteer on a regular basis.

  Credentials/Documentation: The applicant must furnish evidence of: capacity to operate direct community service programs; experience and interest in the needs of older adults; and the ability to develop strong community financial and programmatic support. Nonprofit organizations must furnish: proof of nonprofit status, articles of incorporation and certification of accounting capability. Costs will be determined in accordance with OMB Circulars No. A-21 for educational institutions, No. A-87 for State and local governments, and No. A-122 for non-profit organizations.

APPLICATION AND AWARD PROCESS:

  Preapplication Coordination: Organizations interested in exploring the possibility of developing a local RSVP project should contact the appropriate Corporation for National Service State Program Office. The Corporation for National Service issues application forms to applicants who have established their eligibility. The standard application forms (modified by the Corporation for National Service with OMB approval), as furnished by the Corporation for National Service and required by OMB Circular No. A-102 must be used for this Program. This Program is eligible for coverage under E.O. 12372, "Intergovernmental Review of Federal Programs." An applicant should consult the office or official designated as the single point of contact in his or her State for more information on the process the State requires to be followed in applying for assistance, if the State has selected the Program for review.

Application Procedure: Applications for new projects are submitted to the Corporation for National Service State Program Office with a copy to the State Office on Aging. State Offices on Aging have 45 days to review and make comments on applications. This Program is subject to the provisions of OMB Circular No. A-110 and A-102 for State and local governments.

Award Procedure: Grants are awarded by the Corporation for National Service. States will be notified of awards through the Federal Assistance Awards Data System (FAADS).

Deadlines: Contact the Corporation for National and Community Service State Office for application deadlines.

Range of Approval/Disapproval Time: 120 days after receipt of application by the Corporation for National Service.

Appeals: No formal appeals for denial of initial grant application, but regulations provide for hearings on terminations and suspensions, and opportunity to show cause in cases of denial of refunding.

Renewals: Grant renewal applications, usually required annually, are submitted 120 days prior to the end of the budget period.

ASSISTANCE CONSIDERATIONS:

Formula and Matching Requirements: This Program has no statutory formulas. The RSVP sponsor is responsible for generating needed financial support for the RSVP project from all sources, Federal and non-Federal, including grants, cash and in-kind contributions, to meet the budgeted costs of the project. The sponsor will supplement a Corporation for National Service grant with other support to the fullest extent possible. As a guide to the level of local support expected, 10 percent of the total budget can be required for the first year, 20 percent for the second year, and 30 percent in any subsequent years. The level of local support negotiated may be higher or lower than these figures, as mutually agreed to by the Corporation for National Service and the sponsor, and as justified by local conditions. Sponsors proposing to contribute local support of less than 30 percent of the total project budget for the third or succeeding years must provide the Corporation for National Service with an acceptable written justification for the lower level of support.

Length and Time Phasing of Assistance: Grant support and budget periods are normally for 12 months, with an opportunity to amend each year; funds are released monthly or quarterly, depending on the size of grant.

POST ASSISTANCE REQUIREMENTS:

Reports: Quarterly Financial Status Report, Periodic Project Progress Report, Quarterly Federal Cash Transactions Report, Annual Project Profile and Volunteer Activity Survey.

Audits: Corporation for National Service grants are subject to audit by the Corporation for National Service, the General Accounting Office, other Federal agencies, and contract auditors. In accordance with the provisions of OMB Circular No. A-133, "Audits of States, Local Governments, and Non-Profit Organizations," grantees that receive financial assistance of $300,000 or more a year in Federal awards shall have an audit made in accordance with OMB Circular No. A-133. Grantees that receive between $25,000 and $300,000 a year in Federal awards shall have an audit made in accordance with OMB Circular No. A-133, or in accordance with Federal laws and regulations governing the programs in which they participate.

Records: All financial records for each budget period, including receipts, disbursements, and vouchers for Federal and nonfederal costs, copies of all contracts, personnel records, and job descriptions must be available for a period of three years from date of submission of the Final Financial Status Report.

FINANCIAL INFORMATION:

Account Identification: 44-0103-0-1-506.

Obligations: (Grants) FY 97 $35,286,000; FY 98 est $39,509,000; and FY 99 est $42,530,000.

Range and Average of Financial Assistance: $2,500 to $83,919; $48,550.

PROGRAM ACCOMPLISHMENTS: For fiscal year 1997, over 450,000 older persons participated in the Corporation for National and Community Service and non-Corporation RSVP projects. They contributed over 74,000,000 hours of service to over 57,600 local organizations. Service opportunities continue in intergenerational activities, education, in-home care, consumer education, environmental activities, public safety, and other health and human service activities. To ensure maximum utilization of program resources, RSVP will provide guidance and technical assistance to other agencies to expand opportunities available to older people.

REGULATIONS, GUIDELINES, AND LITERATURE: 45 CFR 1209; Retired and Senior Volunteer Program flyers.

INFORMATION CONTACT:

Regional or Local Office: Corporation for National Service State Program Offices as listed in Appendix IV of the Catalog.

Headquarters Office: National Senior Service Corps, Retired and Senior

Volunteer Program, Corporation for National Service, 1201 New York Avenue, NW Washington, DC 20525. Telephone: (202) 606-5000 ext. 189 and 1-800-424-8867.

RELATED PROGRAMS: 94.011, Foster Grandparent Program; 94.016, Senior Companion Program.

EXAMPLES OF FUNDED PROJECTS: The following exemplifies RSVP: An RSVP service volunteer, who is a retired architect and engineer, designs homes for low-income families displaced by mid-western floods. Another volunteer, who is bilingual, uses her fluency in English and Japanese to help non-English speaking Japanese seniors access community resources and live independently. Another RSVP volunteer is the coordinator, fund-raiser and supervisor of over 30 other RSVP volunteers who operate an inner-city soup kitchen which feeds more than 250,000 homeless and disadvantaged persons annually. In another instance, RSVP volunteers organized neighborhood watches for an entire city of more than 45,000. As a result, the police noted a 58 percent reduction in crime in some areas. RSVP provides creative opportunities for older people to serve their communities by responding to locally identified needs. The following statistics suggest the scope of their service: During fiscal year 1997, over 127,000 RSVP volunteers served at 10,400 acute care hospitals, clinics, and other medical care facilities. Over 30,700 volunteers served in over 6,000 schools. Other volunteers served with police departments, Head Start centers, libraries and ground water protection agencies.

CRITERIA FOR SELECTING PROPOSALS: 1. Demonstrated need for the Program in the community to be served; 2. Evidence of community support for the Program; 3. Goals and objectives that are clear, measurable and time-phased; 4. Assurance that Program requirements will be complied with in a cost-effective manner; 5. The potential sponsor must have the following characteristics: a. The capacity to manage and operate a quality community service volunteer program; b. A good working relationship with other community service agencies and organizations especially those dealing with older persons; c. The capacity to develop sources of non-Federal support; d. A governing body or agency board which understands and endorses the nature and purpose of the Program.

COMPUTER RESOURCES

It is possible to search for a grant source using computer databases. A computer search allows you to combine ideas or terms in your search. A computer searches fast, but it also takes time for you to learn how to use a program effectively. Most people find the reference books easier to use. A majority of the people I have asked told me they found more potential funding sources by using books rather than by using a computer search.

A CD-ROM called *FC Search* has been produced by the Foundation Center. This CD-ROM contains the data found in their major foundation and corporate reference books. Start in the Advanced Grant Maker mode. There is a user manual which you ought to review. It has a list of the index terms used in the CD-ROM so that you will know how to phrase your searches. Also in the manual are instructions on search techniques and examples of effective searching.

Some other CD-ROMs with grants information are the Chronicle of Philanthropy *Guide to Grants*, the Taft Group *Prospector's Choice*, and Aspen Publishers' *GrantScape*. Versions of the these databases may also be available on 3.5" disks.

The Dialog online system, available at many libraries, has grant databases. *The Foundation Directory* (file 26) offers a computerized search for grant makers. The same information is available in Foundation Center books. Searching on Dialog is normally done by librarians, and there are fees incurred in doing the search. Those fees may be passed on to you.

The Foundation Directory is available online for a fee. It is part of the Foundation Center web site. Using the search screen allows a person to locate appropriate foundations.

The Internet has numerous web sites with grant information. The information available on the net is not everything you need. The Internet supplements other resources, but it does not replace them. For example, under 10% of foundations have a web site of their own. A person definitely must use other information resources too. Federal government grant information on the Internet is more complete than for the other grant making sources. Some state and local governments have posted information about their grant programs. The corporate data on the Internet is business, not grant, oriented. *At the back of this book is a 2002 list of the most useful web sites.*

Some net sites have general information about grants and some are specialized. For instance, there is a specialized site (not listed in the appendix) designed by the Society of Research Administrators, http://www. srainternational.org/cws/sra/sra.htm It has information for people doing research studies, and the site focuses on federal grants. Other sites are intended for the use of a variety of grant seekers.

If you have no Internet access that will not keep you from getting a grant. However, many public libraries offer Internet access for free. Using the Internet is not difficult. A primary reason to go online is to review a foundation tax return, as discussed next. The tax return can be obtained in several other ways though.

FOUNDATION TAX RETURNS

When you have selected a few foundations to focus on you ought to examine their federal tax returns, the 990-PF forms, that each foundation must file. These tax returns are by law open to public review. The older returns are on microfilm, and reader-printer machines make paper copies from the microfilm. Newer tax returns are made available on CD-ROMs or the Internet, and can also be printed out. The 990-PF contains fundamental information about a foundation, full financial data, a contact person, and brief application information. **Also shown are all the grants the foundation made**. One part has information about what the foundation does and does not support. These tax returns can add significantly to what you find in books.

Government departments and corporations do not file tax returns that will supply you with grant information. Corporate foundations do file 990-PFs. The PF stands for private foundation, which is the I.R.S. term for almost all foundations. Ignore the word "private." These are foundations the public can interact with.

Don't let the length or seeming complexity of the 990-PF intimidate you. In my on-going quest to make things so simple that even I can understand them, I have found there are just a few parts that you should concentrate on. At the top of page one is the name, address, and phone number of a foundation. Also the value of their assets is shown. (A blank first page of a 990-PF is printed in this book to show you how it looks.) The most important part of the return is presently labeled as Part XV. That part has brief grant application information, and shows each grant made with the recipient, purpose of the grant, and the amount.

Form **990-PF**	**Return of Private Foundation** or Section 4947(a)(1) Nonexempt Charitable Trust Treated as a Private Foundation	OMB No. 1545-0052
Department of the Treasury Internal Revenue Service	Note: *The organization may be able to use a copy of this return to satisfy state reporting requirements.*	**1998**

For calendar year 1998, or tax year beginning _____ , 1998, and ending _____

Use the IRS label. **Otherwise, please print or type.** **See Specific Instructions.**	Name of organization	**A** Employer identification number
	Number and street (or P.O. box number if mail is not delivered to street address) Room/suite	**B** Telephone number (see page 9 of the instructions) ( )
	City or town, state, and ZIP + 4	**C** If exemption application is pending, check here ▶ ☐

H Check type of organization: ☐ Section 501(c)(3) exempt private foundation
☐ Section 4947(a)(1) nonexempt charitable trust ☐ Other taxable private foundation

D 1. Foreign organizations, check here . ▶ ☐
2. Organizations meeting the 85% test, check here and attach computation . ▶ ☐

I Fair market value of all assets at end of year *(from Part II, col. (c), line 16)* ▶ $ _____

J Accounting method: ☐ Cash ☐ Accrual
☐ Other (specify) ....
(Part I, column (d) must be on cash basis.)

E If private foundation status was terminated under section 507(b)(1)(A), check here . ▶ ☐
F If the foundation is in a 60-month termination under section 507(b)(1)(B), check here . ▶ ☐
G If address changed, check here . ▶ ☐

Part I — Analysis of Revenue and Expenses *(The total of amounts in columns (b), (c), and (d) may not necessarily equal the amounts in column (a) (see page 9 of the instructions).)*

		(a) Revenue and expenses per books	(b) Net investment income	(c) Adjusted net income	(d) Disbursements for charitable purposes (cash basis only)
1	Contributions, gifts, grants, etc., received (attach schedule)				
2	Contributions from split-interest trusts				
3	Interest on savings and temporary cash investments				
4	Dividends and interest from securities . . .				
5a	Gross rents				
b	(Net rental income or (loss) _____)				
6	Net gain or (loss) from sale of assets not on line 10				
7	Capital gain net income (from Part IV, line 2) . .				
8	Net short-term capital gain				
9	Income modifications				
10a	Gross sales less returns and allowances				
b	Less: Cost of goods sold . . .				
c	Gross profit or (loss) (attach schedule)				
11	Other income (attach schedule)				
12	**Total.** Add lines 1 through 11				
13	Compensation of officers, directors, trustees, etc.				
14	Other employee salaries and wages				
15	Pension plans, employee benefits				
16a	Legal fees (attach schedule)				
b	Accounting fees (attach schedule)				
c	Other professional fees (attach schedule) . . .				
17	Interest				
18	Taxes (attach schedule) (see page 12 of the instructions)				
19	Depreciation (attach schedule) and depletion .				
20	Occupancy				
21	Travel, conferences, and meetings				
22	Printing and publications				
23	Other expenses (attach schedule)				
24	**Total operating and administrative expenses.** Add lines 13 through 23				
25	Contributions, gifts, grants paid				
26	**Total expenses and disbursements.** Add lines 24 and 25				
27	Subtract line 26 from line 12:				
a	Excess of revenue over expenses and disbursements				
b	Net investment income (if negative, enter -0-) . .				
c	Adjusted net income (if negative, enter -0-) . .				

For Paperwork Reduction Act Notice, see the instructions.   Cat. No. 11289X   Form **990-PF** (1998)

You can learn a great deal from the list of grants made. You can learn whether the foundation has supported any projects similar to your own in subject, in location, in amount, or in type of support.

Foundation tax returns are on file at some cooperating collection libraries and at some very large libraries. It is possible to obtain the tax returns from the Internal Revenue Service. You may also contact a foundation to request its most recent tax returns. As mentioned before some foundations do not have any employees. These unstaffed foundations may be very slow to respond. This is true even though I.R.S. regulations require that a foundation must provide you with the copies.

> GrantSmart, GuideStar, and the Foundation Center are putting copies of 990-PFs on their Internet sites. These free sites and their addresses are listed at the end of this book. Also there are I.R.S. plans to make the tax returns available on the net. These recent advances greatly benefit grant seekers. You can now easily look at the returns and learn about foundation giving patterns. Since searching ability is limited on these net sites, you should first select the foundations to be studied.

Checking the tax returns should be done whenever feasible. The only exception would be when you have gotten enough background already, for instance through research and then contact with a foundation.

GOVERNMENT INFORMATION

For **state and local government grants** there is not much printed or online information. Thus you should make contact with your state and local *elected officials*, and also with the *relevant department in the government* to ask if there is a grant available for what you want to do. For example, you could call the state welfare department at the capital to ask about possible grants for social services. Keep dialing until you reach a person in the know. If one office cannot help you, inquire about what other office might. You should call the offices of your state senator or state representative, your county commissioner, and your mayor. Cover all the bases. Your local library with its directories of government offices can assist you in finding the right names, addresses, and phone numbers.

For **federal grants** you could call the office of your representative in the U.S. Congress. His or her staff will not obtain a grant for you, but they might know of grants available. Many Congressional offices have a staff person who has some federal grants expertise. Before calling the Congressional office, first use the book mentioned next.

To start looking for a federal grant, use the indexes of the *Catalog of Federal Domestic Assistance*. When you find a good lead in the *Catalog of Federal Domestic Assistance*, the next step is to **write or call the listed information contact**.

With a federal or local contact person, ask your questions and get whatever printed material or forms are available for the grant program. The contact person or office will give you a description of the government grant program, advice about your grant project, guidance on how best to submit your request, and an update on the current availability of funds.

At times the *Catalog of Federal Domestic Assistance* will show zero funding available, but that may only mean the funding appropriation was late in being passed and missed the printing deadline. The information contact could tell you that. He or she may also know of similar grant programs that could be of value to you.

Some government departments publish their own lists of available grants. Ask if the department has any newsletters that might have grant leads. You could request to be added to the mailing list.

The *Catalog of Federal Domestic Assistance* aims at containing all the federal grant programs. However, some research grants or small grant programs do not get included. To become aware of the programs not included, contact the department that deals with the issue which concerns you.

The federal government has booklets which explain their grant accounting rules. You could find the rules in Office of Management and Budget Circular A-122, *Cost Principles for Non-Profit Organizations*, and O.M.B. Circular A-110, *Uniform Administrative Requirements for Grants....* You could consult the O.M.B. web site to get these publications and others. It is found at http://www.whitehouse.gov/OMB/grants.

In the future federal agencies will be putting more grant making and grant administration online. Also, federal applications and administration will become more uniform. Electronic funds transfer by the government is already becoming routine.

OTHER HELPFUL RESOURCES

The Grantsmanship Center publishes a free magazine about grant topics that is quite informative. They will send you a subscription to the *Grantsmanship Center Magazine*. This is a good way to continue learning about grants. I urge you to write to them at the following address, on your nonprofit's letterhead stationery: Subscription Department, Grantsmanship Center, P.O. Box 17220, Los Angeles CA 90017. They will mail magazines to your organization's business address only.

Other magazines in the grants field could be of value to you. Some of the better known ones are: *Contributions*, *The Chronicle of Philanthropy*, *Nonprofit Times*, and *Grassroots Fundraising Journal*. You might examine them during your trip to the library. These magazines have instructive articles which over time will teach you more about grants and fund-raising.

Nonprofit organizations which have received grants from a funder who interests you may be a productive source of inside information. You could call the nonprofit to see if the persons involved with the grant will talk about their experiences and share what they learned about working with the funder. Organizations like yours in other cities may tell you about their grant seeking methods.

Libraries have reference books which have various kinds of background information that could be of use to you. For example, there are books that list corporations and indicate what business they are in, the names of executives, the net earnings, and where they do business. That will help with corporate grants. The best way to get started finding corporate data is to ask a librarian for assistance. Libraries are a good source of information for just about any need you have.

PERSONAL CONTACTS

Do as much research on grant makers as possible before making phone calls to them. (Grant makers will expect that.) Always do try to make phone contact because you can learn so much that way.

Don't expect to get a grant by just a phone call. When you call a funder, ask to speak with someone who is familiar with the grant making procedures. With some smaller foundations a trustee may take the lead. For large foundations there could be staff who each specialize by subject. In seeking a corporate grant you want to identify the executive who is in charge of grant making. That individual can tell you about the company's grant policies and procedures. In seeking a government grant, as mentioned before, you want to identify who is responsible for grant applications in your field of interest.

Having found an influential person, you can describe the concept for the grant, ask your questions, and make a favorable impression. Before your call, make a written outline of what matters you want to cover. For all funders, if you don't know, you should ask about:

- the appropriateness of your grant request (subject, location, amount, or type of support),
- whether there are application guidelines, application forms, or materials describing the funder,
- how long your proposal should be,
- what documents they want to see (financial statements? trustee names? other items?),
- funding deadlines,
- what the most common mistakes they see are.

At times funders will not be willing to talk on the phone about your proposal. Also, you may not be able to find a phone number for smaller foundations. In that last case, of course, you would write to ask for the information you need.

Some grant sources print their guidelines. Guidelines are the procedures and giving policies of a grant source. Always ask a grant source for guidelines. Unfortunately, many foundations do not print application information or basic guidelines that inform you of what they fund and how to apply. Corporations tend to publish application information. The government usually does supply an application packet.

In your research you may come across the term, "letter of inquiry." This term is used to mean different things by different people. It could be a letter you send asking for background information about a funder, or a letter you send summarizing a grant proposal. Despite the ambiguity, you should always get background information about a funder first. Then you should decide whether to send a grant proposal using a letter format or a document format.

There are funders who prefer not to meet with grants seekers. It's too much like sitting down with a salesman. It would take a lot of time for a funder to meet with all grant seekers.

Some grant makers (usually smaller foundations with no staff) might be unresponsive to your request for information about them. One trustee might be getting all the mail for a smaller foundation and be overburdened and not reply. Getting no reply is a real problem. Because of the research methods referred to in this chapter, you will have been able to find out a great deal about the grant maker anyway. Based on what you know, you might believe there is a good match between the funder's interests and your organization's interests. So you may want to go ahead with trying more phone or mail contacts.

> For grants in Canada, take a look at this useful web site, "Canada Grants Service" which describes grant research materials.
> http://www.interlog.com/~cgs/

RESEARCH

Research helps you in several ways. In addition to selecting a source of funding, you will be better prepared to write the grant request, and to work with the funder.

> Remember to do the following. Check the relevant foundation 990-PF. Make personal contact with a funding source. Employ the funder identification work sheet.

Your grant is important to you. It is important to the people you help. Helen Keller believed that, "Although the world is full of suffering, it is also full of the overcoming of it." Your organization, through your actions, can reduce personal suffering. A grant is an opportunity to further your goals.

You will not secure each and every grant you aim for, however you will get some. The grants you do obtain make it very much worthwhile to keep trying. And when you have brought home some grants, there is a crucial step that should follow. You walk into the office of your supervisor and say, "Hi! I've been so busy bringing in substantial grants for our organization that I haven't had a chance to talk with you about my salary level. What's a good time for you?"

In an effort to be comprehensive, I know I have made the research seem more complicated than it is. Once you start, this research will seem easy to do. It may not even take more than one trip to the library to obtain a grant.

Give yourself a really good chance of getting a grant by doing the work of research well. That leads to success. It does take a bit of effort to do the research, but it pays off. Good research is vital. Well, there is an alternative. You could always consult a psychic... but I would make that a second choice.

WHAT TO DO NOW

First, make a list of the largest foundations in your area. Let's say within about 30 miles of where your organization is located. Then read about and evaluate these funders, selecting the ones with the potential to help you. This selective prospect list will be useful now and over the next few years. The list will probably contain your **best options** for grants. Use *The Foundation Directory* and *The Foundation Directory Part 2* to compile your foundation prospect list. These books have a geographic index in the back section that shows foundations by state and city. Then, use the subject index to find other foundations making grants for what you want to do.

Chapter 4

HOW TO WRITE AN EFFECTIVE GRANT REQUEST

"Genius that power which dazzles mortal eyes
is often perseverance in disguise."
C. C. Cameron

When he was the Governor of Arkansas, Bill Clinton, addressed a grants conference there. After the meeting he spoke with several of the people attending, and then offered to take them the next day on a tour around Arkansas. Clinton said, "I'll show you this state, I'm the best guide in all of Arkansas." Arrangements were made to get Clinton's limousine, and he drove them on the trip. After a few hours though, it appeared to some of the persons that Clinton was completely lost. Eventually he pulled over and stopped. One of the persons said to Clinton, "It looks like we're wandering aimlessly. You said you're the best guide in all of Arkansas." "Well," said Clinton, pausing for a moment, "I am… but I think we're in Texas now."

My job is to keep you out of Texas, so to speak.

Let's look at how to write a grant proposal which will bring you the grant money you need. A sample grant proposal follows this chapter. There are several basic ideas to keep in mind during the writing process.

One of the decisive factors that brings success in getting a grant is *the effort invested*. People who invest their time produce better work and are rewarded accordingly. I know you do not want to spend a lot of time writing the grant proposal. However, I should point out that grant makers can tell the difference between two proposals, one a rush job and the other a polished product.

Look at the proposal from *the perspective of donors*. How will they view the request? What would you look at if you were evaluating a grant request? I would consider matters such as whether the proposed grant would accomplish something valuable, has a reasonable budget, and is submitted by an organization in which I have confidence. Funders may not intuitively realize why it's important that you receive the grant. In writing the grant request remember that the persons evaluating your request may not understand technical terms you use every day, or even understand what your organization does. You need to start from scratch in your explanations. In doing so, don't use words or abbreviations the average reader will not be familiar with.

Emphasize your credibility as an effective organization. *Building confidence and trust in your organization is critical.* Show that you are a "can do" team, which because of your strengths can do the project well if given funding. What could you write that will highlight your professionalism, past successes, and special abilities? Indicating something of your history and achievements, the positive stories of persons whom you helped, or the qualifications of your staff builds confidence. Grant makers usually fund stable organizations of proven effectiveness. Many grant makers don't like to take risks by investing in financially troubled organizations. If you were about to invest in a company, you would check out the company. Grantors will do the same with their investments in nonprofit organizations. You give your own donations to organizations you trust. Grant makers give to organizations they trust. One major part of getting a grant is establishing a relationship of trust.

It's important to *highlight the benefits you can realistically achieve*. This is a vital aspect of a proposal. The proposal ought to have a compelling answer to the question: why should this grant be made? Your answer is: because the benefits to be gained are significant. Then you elaborate on that. You can't save the whole world, but you can make it much better for some persons in some ways. You do not have to promise unrealistic improvements. The proposal may not be taken seriously if you do. Another reason to be realistic is that you will later evaluate whether the goals were actually achieved. So do not set goals you really cannot reach.

Be specific in describing your grant project from start to finish. Vague statements in your proposal will raise questions, rather than answering them. Often the person reading your proposal will not ask, or be in a position to ask, questions about your grant request. This may mean it is rejected because of open questions which could have been answered quite well. **Anticipate the questions and objections which a reviewer might have**. Write your responses into the proposal. With the initial request put in all the information you wish to be considered. There may not be the opportunity to add anything later.

Follow all the instructions given to you by the funding organization. Some funders (mostly government funders) weed out and reject grant requests based solely on the fact that some of the instructions were not followed. They sit down with grant proposals and divide them into two stacks. One stack has complete proposals with the instructions followed, and is set aside for further consideration. The other stack has major omissions or errors... and is not considered. It is very important, therefore, to know what the funding organization wants, and to send them what they want. Following the instructions of the funding organization also raises your credibility. Grant makers might wonder, if a nonprofit does not follow our basic directions now, can we rely on that nonprofit in more complicated matters in the future? When a funding source requests specific information, provide all that information. If the grant maker wants items A,B,C,D write about A,B,C,D... not C,B,D. When you integrate what is requested into the body of the proposal, use underlines, bold print, or headings to make the requested information stand out. Following the instructions of the funding source may sound obvious, but there are grant seekers who will not do that. You will have an advantage over them.

When you learn what a funder wants you can improve your chance of getting a grant by making adjustments that *tailor your proposal* to what the funder wants. While composing a proposal you can get better results if you **"echo back"** what the funding source says it wants. If a corporate funder states, we want the use of proven methods by experienced organizations, then you write about your use of proven methods by your experienced organization. You respond directly to the funder's concerns by speaking their language.

Don't plead in your proposal, or try to make a funder feel guilty about not providing a grant. For one thing, it doesn't work. Also, an overly emotional appeal may leave a bad taste in the mouth of a funder which you may want to approach in the future. Not getting a grant this time, does not mean there won't be other grants received from that source later on.

For general reference, here are some common gripes of grant funders I have heard over the years. Funders don't appreciate:

- cold calls on the phone which reveal the caller doesn't know anything about the grant maker,
- your sending the same request for grant money to several funding sources simultaneously,
- getting grant requests for a kind of grant the funder does not provide,

- proposals that are not clearly written, as in, "We read your proposal, but we don't quite get it."
- vague assertions about what the grant may accomplish,
- lack of honesty on the part of grant seekers,
- failure to follow through after the grant is made, with what was promised,
- receiving another grant request right after the funder just made a grant to your organization.

What are the basic reasons people don't get grants? One typical grant maker has said proposals do not get funded because, "The project is outside our guidelines, the quality of the project is poor, and/or the cost per client served is unacceptably high." "Outside our guidelines" means that the request is for something the grant maker does not fund.

Over the years, I have discovered a frequent reason people don't get grants. They never put a request for a grant in a mailbox. No request... no grant.

LETTER PROPOSALS AND DOCUMENT PROPOSALS

There are two ways to present your grant request. The basic proposal formats are a letter, or a longer document format. A letter of about *two or three pages* (if single-spaced and without an appendix) asking for a grant is appropriate when the funding source indicates to send a letter first. A few funders even ask for a letter of only one page to get things started. Your research will tell you what they want. A longer letter is to your advantage because you can make a more complete case for funding. The letter proposal content follows the proposal outline described in this chapter. You might write two or three paragraphs on each of the first seven proposal sections. Check to see if the funder wants any of the items normally added in the *appendix* section. The letter format is the same as **a standard business letter** on your letterhead paper. Sometimes this letter is called a "letter of intent," "a query letter," or a "preliminary letter."

Because the letter proposal is briefer than the document proposal, it saves both you and the funder some time. The persons who look over grant requests have more than enough reading matter. You can benefit from easier preparation and a faster response. On the negative side, you might have just one chance to make an impression with each potential grantor and a short letter proposal may not do full justice to your request. When there is no information about what a funder requests, or when the funder requests "a proposal" *use the document proposal format* described next.

A document proposal has between *three to ten pages*. That is not counting the appendix, and when it is single-spaced. Always use only one side of the paper. The document proposal, sometimes called a "full proposal," comprehensively describes all the details of your grant project.

A one page cover letter in a normal business style goes with the document proposal to introduce it. The cover letter has a sentence or two on each of the following: need, goals, benefits, plan, and cost. The cover letter includes the main reasons the grant should be made.

In a cover letter or a letter proposal indicate if you will need the funds by a certain time. Also say if you are approaching other funding sources about this proposal, and explain.

You conclude in either a cover letter or a letter proposal by offering to answer any questions, and requesting a meeting about the proposal. Often the funding organization will not want a meeting, but you should suggest the idea. If a meeting is held that's a very good opportunity to sell your project. Meetings will be for clarification and general discussion of the written proposal.

A document proposal may need to be written even after sending a letter proposal because most grantors will expect to see detailed information before they make a final decision. The longer proposal version shows you have done your homework, and helps you in planning for the use of the grant.

Usually the larger the amount of money sought, the longer the proposal is. If you want ten thousand dollars, a shorter proposal is more appropriate. If you want a quarter of a million dollars, you've got some explaining to do. Some subjects require longer explanations. A proposal for a medical research grant will be inherently much more technical and lengthy than a proposal for a couple of new personal computers. Write as much as necessary to completely and convincingly present your request.

As far as the maximum length of the proposal is concerned, my theory is this, a person who is asleep cannot make a grant to you. There are no reported exceptions to this theory. The bottom line is that the proposal should be concise, but detailed enough to present the best case for funding your request. A reasonable maximum length is generally ten pages when single-spaced. The appendix may add many more pages. Government grant proposals may be much longer than ten pages because of their special requirements. How long should your particular proposal be? It should be **long enough to say what you really want to say**.

Another basic question is, how much money should you ask for? **Ask for what you really need**. It takes about as much work to get a $50,000 grant as it does to get a $40,000 grant.

The proposal should be personalized to address the interests of the grant maker. Because each grantor is somewhat unique, **they may have their own forms**, or a proposal style they want you to use. You learn that through research. Of course, what the funder wants takes precedence over the standard practices we will cover. With the proposal on a computer you can easily modify the proposal to fit a particular funder's requests.

> Send your proposal to the president of a foundation's board, or to whomever else is designated, as shown by your research. Address your request to a person, rather than "To whom it may concern."

Your cover letter or letter proposal ought to be signed by the president of your board of trustees, or your chief administrator. This is good form and that individual may have name recognition in the community. Also, occasionally an enterprising person has tried to get a grant without telling the top management of a nonprofit. What could have been a wonderful surprise soured a bit, when the administrators once again discovered that they didn't know what was going on in their own organization. Make the grant a good experience. Let the administrators know what you are doing so you get credit for trying to help, whether you get a grant or not.

You may want to list a knowledgeable individual as the person to contact with questions if the letter signer is not well informed about the grant request. For example, "Mr. Bob Black (429-3385 ext. 105) is managing this grant project and is the best person to answer specific questions about it."

The document proposal format has eight sections which might be labeled in capitals with a few lines of space between the sections. Each of the first seven sections has several paragraphs of explanation. The last section is the appendix. The proposal example at the end of this chapter is a document proposal. (Take a couple of minutes to scan through it now so you will have an idea of what a proposal looks like.)

A title page after the cover letter shows: your organization's name, address, phone number, the project title, "A Proposal Submitted To _____," and the date. Putting a table of contents page next for a long proposal can be very helpful to the reader. The details regarding appearance and typing style are matters of taste. They are up to you, unless the funder provides specific directions.

In writing the proposal use short simple sentences for ease of understanding. Do not expatiate in phraseology of abstruse complexity. What I mean to say is… write clearly. A person reading your proposal may go through it rapidly. When you want a point to stand out, make it stand out visually also. Bullet points, boxes with print, and other highlighting methods come in handy.

Double-spacing is at times requested by grant makers, and some of them may insist on it. Personally I believe that content matters a whole lot more than typing style, but I also believe in giving funders what they ask for.

In the document proposal number the pages. In your writing direct the reader's attention to any important items contained in the appendix, so they won't be overlooked.

By the way, funders consistently prefer not to receive videotapes. The tapes are cumbersome to circulate among the different persons evaluating the proposal, and the tapes take too much time to view at a grants distribution committee meeting.

Let's consider the eight section proposal format, section by section. This proposal format is a tested method of asking for grant money. It has worked for many people seeking grants from all types of funders. This commonly used format has all the basic elements you need to include in a proposal. The sections and the questions they answer are:

1. Summary: What is this all about? Why is action required?
2. Our Organization: Who is going to do this?
3. Need: What is the concern to be addressed?
4. Goals and Benefits: What are the expected positive outcomes? Where?
5. Plan: How are the goals and benefits going to be achieved? When?
6. Evaluation: Were the goals and benefits achieved?
7. Cost: How much is this going to cost?
8. Appendix: What other information supports the request?

So you will have answered the fundamental questions: who, what, when, where, why, how, and how much. There is a **logical sequence in the proposal**, each section builds upon the others. For instance, you indicate the need, then what you want to do about the need, then how you will do that.

SUMMARY

The first step is the summary. Well, actually, the first two steps are to worry and to procrastinate. But assuming you've already done that... you can now go into the summary. It is a brief review of your grant request. The summary must be good, because it may be the only part that is read! If the funder doesn't like what is written here, he may not go any farther. So take your best shot up front. The summary gives you the opportunity to *highlight* what you believe are the most important aspects of your proposal

It has been said that the main thing is to make the main thing, the main thing. That is what you should do in the summary, write about the main points. *Include at least a sentence or two on each of these items: need, goals, benefits, plan, and amount requested.*

Since the cover letter for a document proposal may not be distributed to all the decision-makers, you need to restate any key points from it in the summary. Use slightly different wording to avoid sounding too repetitive. In the shorter letter style proposal, the summary may be the first paragraph of the letter. Sometimes a summary is called an abstract.

If you can't think of any other way to start the proposal, you can begin with, "It was a dark and stormy night." That always works for me.

OUR ORGANIZATION

The second section, our organization, is the description of your nonprofit organization. Even supposedly well-known groups, such as the American Heart Association, have many functions which most of us are not aware of. Your nonprofit is much the same. Can you name three services of the American Heart Association? Can the average person name three services of your organization? Most people outside your organization don't know what it really does. (Some people inside your organization don't know what it really does.) The persons reading your proposal do not fully appreciate what you do; in the both the sense that they do not understand, and therefore they do not accurately value your contribution to the public welfare. Here is where you create an understanding of how much you add to the lives of the people you assist.

State your organizational mission, basic activities, what group you help, the number of people helped, geographic service area, and organizational size. Additionally you might supply brief information about your physical facility or your history. Include information about aspects of your nonprofit that are especially relevant to the grant. I know it would take pages of narrative to do justice to your organization, however be selective about what you include.

Focus on your strengths and abilities. Show that your organization is clearly capable of administering this grant program effectively. This is a nice place to mention relevant past successes and major achievements. Has the organization received any awards or good evaluations? Is the organization accredited, licensed, or certified? Are there any impressive statistics you can cite, such as, you are the largest provider of a certain type of service in the county, or your results exceed state averages? If you want to prove to someone that your nonprofit is effective, how could you do that? Your chief objective in this section is to build confidence, to show that yours is an organization which can be relied upon.

If you were going to give away a large sum of money, you would want to know that it would be spent by capable people. For most grants one person or a few persons will be managing the use of the grant, and those persons are key factors in the success of the grant. You might want to spotlight the qualifications, experience, and achievements of the staff who will be working directly with the grant funds. You could add even more about the staff, such as their resumes, in the appendix.

For new organizations which cannot refer to a track record, concentrate on the strengths you currently have. You could also elaborate on the importance of your goals, your early successes, the experience of your staff, leaders, or trustees, your organizational progress, and what gives your grant plan a significant chance of success. For organizations with financial problems, don't bring that up unless the problem is obvious. If that issue is obvious or comes up, point to the progress being made, the importance of your mission, and signs of organizational stability. Perhaps you could work in partnership with a more established organization.

The comfort factor is important when dealing with large amounts of money. You want to make the donor comfortable about giving you money to fund your plan. Some plans sound great on paper, but never work out, you know how that is. All grant makers have had the memorable experience of seeing their grants produce little of value because the fine sounding goals were never really attained. You should give the reader a sense of trust in your agency. Build trust by emphasizing your organization's abilities.

NEED

The description of the need is the third section. What is the nature of the need to be addressed by the grant? Who has the need? How bad is the situation? What is the cause of the problem? What are the *consequences*, what does the unmet need lead to? If you have an organizational need, how does that affect the people you serve? Your proposal should answer these questions. Demonstrate that the need exists in your local area. What evidence proves the need exists? Quotes, news articles, studies, or expert opinions might be cited to make your case. Lengthy background material should go in the appendix, but could be summarized.

> Judiciously used, statistics will validate the need. A few "wow" type statistics are more productive than a string of numbers. When using statistics include the sources of the data.

You ought to describe briefly the relevant personal, social, economic, physical, or mental characteristics of the people you will help. You could also relate the personal story of someone to put the need on a more human level, to illustrate the situation, and to have more impact. That is known as putting a face with the story.

You can employ both convincing logic and emotion here. Use logic and emotion in that order. A little emotional feeling will draw the reader into the story you are telling. A little too much will detract from the professional image you want to present. Just as you are influenced by a touch of sadness when hearing of personal suffering, so are grant makers. You could insert some interesting quotes, or relate the experiences of people affected by your organization.

At times, one person's story can represent the circumstances of many other persons. As in, "Nothing makes the point as clearly as the story of Bonnie...." A brief sad story or a brief success story could contribute impact to your narrative. Leave the reader with an understanding of what it feels like to be a person with the need.

Can you think of someone who has already been helped in ways the grant will help other people? You might use that person as an illustration. However, don't rely on just that alone. Facts about the whole group of people helped cannot be left out. Grant makers tend to be a very rational bunch, and you will not be convincing unless you concentrate on making a solid reasonable case for the grant.

GOALS AND BENEFITS

Following the description of the need comes your indication of the outcomes you want from the grant, to respond to the need. The goals and benefits section is the statement of what you intend to achieve.

Goals are what your organization wants to attain with the grant. *Goals are desired, specific, and measurable.* You might have multiple goals or one goal. Your goal might be to teach certain concepts, or to provide a service. Achieving the goal will result in benefits for the people you help.

Don't promise what you can't deliver. Narrow down the goals to something you can deal with in a reasonable time with reasonable resources.

What changes exactly are you going to bring about? Who will change? How? How much? How many people will be assisted? What locations will be affected? To stimulate your thinking you might ask yourself, how are things now, and how should they be?

Being specific is good, and means using numerical statements when possible. Quantify the goals. To illustrate, which goal is more specific and communicates the most?

1. We will provide many unemployed older workers with valuable educational training they do not have.
2. We will tutor 120 unemployed persons over age 55 who do not have high school diplomas. Three-fourths of them will pass the General Educational Development Test for a high school equivalency diploma within six months.

Number two would be looked at more favorably by grant makers. It sets a standard by which success can be measured. With number one, it's so vague you won't know whether the goal was actually reached or not. Are your grant goals SMART? Specific, Measurable, Appropriate, Realistic, Thought-out.

Elaborate on the benefits to be gained from the grant and why they are significant. Your proposal ought to indicate not just what will happen, but all of the benefits which follow from that. The goals are the **targets for your organization**. The benefits are the **advantages created for the people you served**, because the targets were met. They are not the same. The goals are what you want to do. The benefits are the positive results from reaching the goals. Benefits are *the good which ultimately comes from the grant*. Some examples of benefits are good health, or economic self-sufficiency. These benefits should be stated more specifically than this at some point in a proposal. The number of persons affected and exactly how they benefit ought to be presented.

Let's think about benefits. Here is an example you as a consumer may have personal experience with. If you go automobile shopping one of your goals may be to get a car with an air conditioner. What you really want is not automotive equipment. You are buying comfort. That comfort is the resulting benefit of the air conditioner purchase.

As in good salesmanship, you should state in a proposal not only what objects or services the grant money is going to buy, but also the benefits which follow. For instance, getting new computers for a school is not in itself a benefit. The *real benefits* are that students learn more in school, they gain skills that enable them to learn in the future, and the students are better prepared to get high tech jobs. The computers are *a means* to bring about the desired benefits. Simply buying hardware may leave a funder cold, be sure to show the consequences of the grant, the human side, the personal benefits ultimately gained. In almost every case what you purchase with grant money is a means to an end. The end result is what you really want. You want the benefits that occur in health, education, or personal improvement.

An effective proposal not only describes, it sells the reader on the importance of the goals and benefits. Focus on who will benefit and how. The benefits that occur in the lives of individuals are the strongest case for funding your grant plan. Include all the major benefits resulting from the grant, and why they are significant. Grant makers will zero in on *why* the grant should be made. So you should too. On a blank sheet of paper, **compose a list of all the reasons why the grant should be made**. Drop any that are trivial and put the rest in the proposal, with the greatest emphasis on the most important reasons.

Sometimes people mistakenly mix the plan in with the goals. The goals are what you want to do, and the plan is how you will do that. In a proposal it works best to deal with one, then the other.

PLAN

The plan is a key section of the proposal because the plan explains **the methods used** to attain the goals and benefits. Try to show your plan to best advantage by being clear and logical. You should describe the fundamental aspects of your plan. There should be enough detail so that a grant maker can understand the basics. With a government grant more detail is usually expected than with grants from other sources.

When there will be large expenditures for human or physical resources, those should be mentioned in the plan. That way a reader can understand why they are necessary, and will therefore appear later in the cost section.

The staff needed for your plan, and their duties, should be explained. Give the name of the individual managing the grant program. Show the titles and hours of the employees involved in the grant program. For instance, you could state that there will be a new career counselor working twenty hours a week to administer the program, assisted with ten hours of clerical support from the present staff. Volunteer hours which are necessary ought to be mentioned, so it is apparent how all the work will be done. Otherwise it will seem that there are jobs to do and no one assigned to do them.

A *time frame* for action should be stated to help clarify the plan. When will you start and when will you finish? For example, you could say that you will begin two months after the grant is received and that the program will run for a total of ten months. A more detailed plan such as for a federal grant, might require a list of the major activities to occur in month one, month two, and so on.

State how you will **publicize the donor's contribution**. Will you have a press release, a recognition ceremony, a plaque, perhaps an article in your newsletter? As noted before, corporate givers especially are concerned about publicity.

Try not to use words such as we "might" or we "may" do something. Demonstrate firmer planning than that. Words that sound uncertain or vague imply that your plan is not finished.

Indicating why your plan will be effective is appropriate. Grant makers are concerned about achieving results. An effective plan is crucial to persuade the potential grantor that your request is a wise investment.

A person can anticipate some of the questions a grant maker will have about any grant plan. One is whether the grant will be used productively. Looking at what is to be spent, is the money really going to produce benefits worth the cost? Cost per person served is an important figure in determining that.

All grant makers like to be assured their funds will be used *effectively* and *efficiently*. There is a distinction between effectiveness and efficiency. If all the goals and benefits were attained, that was an effective program. If all the goals and benefits were attained, but at twice the projected reasonable cost, that was not an efficient program.

EVALUATION

The way to determine the effectiveness and efficiency of the grant program is to have an evaluation. An evaluation is standard practice. Grant makers will normally expect an evaluation. **The evaluation reviews the goals and benefits to find out the degree to which they were achieved, and at what cost. Tests, questionnaires, interviews, surveys, sampling, tracking progress toward a goal**, or otherwise studying changes in the people you helped through the grant are types of evaluation.

As with the other sections of the proposal, the evaluation should be more extensive for a large grant, which stands to reason. You will be expected to show more accountability with a large grant.

The evaluation assists you because you learn from this feedback, and you can tell if changes in your program are needed for the future. Evaluation helps to achieve a high quality program.

Good evaluation should gather information, and analyze that information. Evaluation should go beyond just reporting factual outcomes into understanding why these outcomes occurred, and the significance of the outcomes. The meaning of the facts may not be obvious. *Interpretation of the facts* is necessary to truly understand what happened.

Designing and Describing the Evaluation

To design and describe the evaluation for the proposal, you need to identify what evidence or data will show the extent to which the goals and benefits were reached. In what way can your results be proven statistically? How will you personally know the level of success in reaching the goals and benefits?

To give the evaluation a structure you might consider each goal and benefit, then consider how to measure each one. Write down the fundamental procedures to make each measurement. Those procedures are the evaluation methods.

Here are a few questions to consider. Answering the questions which follow will assist in the planning of your evaluation process. *Write the answers into the proposal.*

- *Who* will make the evaluation?
- *What* will be measured?
- *How* will that be measured?
- *When* will the evaluation take place?

The evaluation is best if it is objective, specific, and quantitative (that is, stated in numbers). It is not very meaningful to say in a lot of words what boils down to, "We spent the $25,000 grant, and we feel good about what happened." That's nice. But what was actually accomplished? If you deposited $25,000 in a bank, would you want to get a statement from the bank later that only said, "we feel good" about what happened with your money?

To use quantitative evaluation makes what you are saying more clear and more precise. Just about any evaluation is easy to state numerically or statistically. For example, a nonprofit might provide employment counseling for 52 unemployed persons with a history of drug abuse. Through interviews three months after the program ends, the counselors learn that 34 of the persons assisted (65% of the total) can show they are now employed. The 65% success rate clarifies what happened. Other results from the interviews could be presented statistically to indicate other outcomes from the grant.

When you design the evaluation during the initial stages of planning, you can gather data to *document a starting point*, and prove that progress has been made toward reaching the goals and benefits. For instance, if you are working with a program to reduce the rate of pregnancy for unmarried teenagers, did the rate of pregnancy go down measurably from the level of previous years?

If you review your program as it goes along, then *you can make mid-course adjustments to improve it*. If the project is already operating, state the results so far.

At times grantors, especially the government, will tell you what to evaluate. They will then review the evaluation and your use of the grant.

Doing the Evaluation

If you are working with a very large number of persons, you might want to evaluate a representative sample of them. That will save your time.

If you just buy equipment, then you need to indicate the extent to which the expected goals and benefits were realized. That evaluation might be brief. Evaluation of a program, on the other hand, is by its nature more involved and lengthy.

Some difficulties may arise that you should be aware of. It may not be possible during a short-term study to evaluate long-term goal achievement, or the benefits that will ultimately occur. Also, watch out for factors not connected to the grant funded program that may influence the outcomes.

If you want to find an objective outside evaluator, college and university faculties are a fine reservoir of evaluators since they have expertise and independence. They might be used for a big or complex grant program. To do a self-evaluation using only your own staff is *the normal practice.*

Try to *keep the evaluation process simple.* Please don't get yourself bogged down in an overly intricate or expensive evaluation process.

Reporting the Evaluation

After the grant is spent you should report your results. You could start the report with a summary of the grant program. State the basic facts: the number of people assisted, the efforts to help them, etc. Summarize how you conducted the evaluation. You could then answer the following basic questions.

- Did the program go as planned?
- To what degree were the goals and benefits achieved?
- What numerical data demonstrates the achievements?
- Why did the results turn out as they did?
- What is the significance of the results?
- What was the final cost?
- What is the future of the grant funded program?

In most situations your grant project does not have to achieve 100% of the set goals to be considered successful. When there are significant improvements, that is progress.

Keep the records from the evaluation. They may be useful in the future.

If you have learned something that could benefit groups like yours, you may want to disseminate what you learned. When other nonprofits can benefit from hearing about your experiences and results that makes your grant program more valuable. You might write an article about your program, or mail the evaluation to similar agencies.

Doing an evaluation of the use of the grant shows accountability and responsibility. Those two qualities will impress funders. Always indicate to each funder that you will send a final evaluation report. Reporting the evaluation results can be used as a way to demonstrate to the funder the level of success, and it's a chance one more time to say thanks for the grant. That type of reinforcement will be quite useful to you in the future because it creates goodwill with the funder.

COST

The cost section displaying how the grant will be spent is next to last. This section not only lists dollar amounts, it clarifies the nature of the grant request. To see where the money is going is to see what the grant is really all about.

A budget is a plan which guides you and commits you to spending the funds for specific purposes. Include a **written narrative** explaining how the project funds will be spent, and a **numerical budget** showing expense categories and their dollar costs.

Your organization can choose to pay for some of the expenses, or ask for a grant equal to 100% of all the program expenses. Clearly *indicate the portion of the total program expenses to be paid by this grant and the portion to be paid by your organization, or some other funding source.* If you plan to ask two or more foundations to fund some part of your plan, indicate the foundations and the amounts. State the already committed funding amounts.

Sometimes getting a grant commitment acts as a stamp of approval which encourages other funding sources to get on board. When foundation A sees that foundation B has already committed to support you, foundation A will tend to think your grant program has been checked out and is probably good.

Do not use a lot of guesses for the expenses. If you do, you may be asking for less than you really need, and could have gotten. It also detracts from the credibility of the budget to show all nice round numbers that are obviously guesses. You know that actual expenses will not come out to exactly $5,000 or $1,000 very often. So do funders. In a few cases, you will have to estimate, but these should be thoughtful accurate estimates.

For example, there could be *income generated by the grant project.* There may be revenue from participant fees. Show the income, and how it will be used. This will have to be an estimate.

Do not add a special budget line for inflation or contingencies. Inflation is relatively low now. If one expense goes up a bit, you could cut back in some other budget area, or add in some of your organization's funds. You can avoid a problem if you do not understate your budget. Likewise, do not unfairly inflate the budget by asking for more than is necessary to accomplish the grant project. Know what funds you will realistically need.

Add a written explanation for any items in the cost section which may be questioned, or which may not be easily understood. (If you plan to fly to Hawaii to conduct two weeks of strategic planning, that may seem to you to be a perfectly logical thing to do, though it will take some explaining.)

There should be enough clarification so that a person not familiar with your organization can understand how each of the figures was arrived at. Be sure to keep any worksheets you prepare so that *you* can understand how each of the figures was arrived at.

Part of the cost section is the numerical budget with prices for all the categories of expenses. It is not necessary to show itemized prices for each and every purchase. For example, a person doesn't need to list each box of paper clips. An office supply budget line that is a reasonable amount will be sufficient. If it looks like minutia to you, lump the expense in with something else. Do not include unidentified expenses, such as "miscellaneous" expenses.

Each budget line could include a brief explanation of the calculation of the expense, as in the budget example which follows in a few pages. Budget categories could be like the ones in the example.

You include direct and possibly indirect costs. *Direct costs* are expenses that apply *only* to the grant program. If an expense occurs solely to support the grant objectives, it is a direct cost. The majority of grant related expenses are direct costs. A new personal computer purchased specifically for the grant project is a direct cost. Payment to a program director to work only with the grant funded program applies just to the operation of the grant program and is a direct cost. On the other hand, paying a bookkeeper who handles both grant and non-grant record keeping is an indirect cost

The *indirect costs* your organization pays to subsidize the implementation of the grant might be reimbursed through the grant. This can be a benefit to your organization. The concept of indirect expenses requires some explanation. Indirect costs are expenses *shared* by both your organization and the grant project. Indirect costs are expense categories which apply to both your usual operation and the grant program also. Indirect costs might include: floor space, utilities, equipment usage, insurance, maintenance, bookkeeping, secretarial services, administration, etc. The federal government may call indirect costs "facilities and administration costs." Indirect costs are something like the overhead costs of a business.

I would guess that only one of ten grants includes indirect costs. **The average grant budget should not use indirect costs**. However, in case you do need to know about indirect costs, I have included this explanation.

To identify indirect costs, ask yourself what your organization is contributing to the operation of the grant program. How is your nonprofit subsidizing the grant activities? In a grant budget you might add in a calculated percentage (say an extra 9%) to cover the administrative, accounting, clerical, and building maintenance expenses of your organization. Being reimbursed for indirect costs means the grant will cover all the real costs of the grant project.

Some indirect costs could be calculated as either indirect or direct costs. For instance floor space is shown in the budget example as a separate itemized cost with the direct costs, but could have been treated as an indirect cost. **Whenever it can be done without difficulty treat costs as direct costs, with each expense category listed on a different line**.

A person could calculate the direct cost for each one of the indirect cost components and itemize each cost separately. Each component expense would be stated on a separate budget line, just like the other direct costs. To get the direct costs for personnel expenses, you would figure the percent of time each person involved will devote to the grant project, and list that percent of the person's salary and benefits as a grant expense. For instance you could budget 25% of an individual's salary and benefit expenses during six months. If a dozen people are involved that would involve many calculations. *Grouping indirect costs together* may simplify the calculations, which is why that is sometimes done. Likewise if there are a multitude of building related costs, such as with a university or other large institution, an indirect cost calculation could simplify matters.

The computation of indirect costs is usually figured as a percentage of direct costs. If your accountant determines that for every $100 spent directly assisting the people you help, your nonprofit must spend another $8 in various administrative expenses, the indirect cost percentage is therefore 8% of direct costs. If total direct costs for the grant are $50,000, then your indirect costs are reasonably accepted as 8%, an additional $4,000. Normally that is 8% of the direct costs you are requesting from the funder, not including any direct costs you will be paying.

> To summarize, the organization's relevant indirect costs are totaled and divided by all the organization's direct costs to create a percentage. Use that percentage of the requested direct costs in the grant budget as the indirect cost amount.

For help with this computation, ask the person who handles the accounting for your nonprofit. He or she will be familiar with the concept.

Keep the indirect cost percentage reasonable. Ten to fifteen percent is at the high end of a normal range. To use a percent above about fifteen percent will seem unacceptable to many foundation and corporate funders, even though your actual costs may be greater. Federal indirect cost rates may well be allowable at higher percentages.

If you are only buying equipment or asking for a general operating grant (one that will be used for your normal yearly expenses) there will be few, or no indirect costs. In some other grant situations there will be only brief, or minor indirect costs. In those situations you should not ask for any indirect cost reimbursement. Only include indirect costs if those costs will be significant, and necessary to carry out the grant program.

It is important to know that **many grant makers will not pay for indirect costs**. Check the policy of the specific funder about getting reimbursed for indirect costs before you request reimbursement for those costs. Remember funding sources act differently, just as individuals do. The federal government often does negotiate an indirect cost rate to reimburse you. A substantial number of foundations or corporations will not like the idea of paying for your indirect costs. They will consider paying these costs as your organization doing its fair share to make the grant program happen.

With government grants be sure you know what the government will and will not pay for. Often there are very specific rules about how to handle grant costs.

Some grant makers will expect your organization to match part of their grant contribution. Indirect costs might be considered as your matching funds, which benefits your organization. (Again, if you find this indirect costs concept too complex or not applicable, use only direct costs.)

An example of a grant budget follows next. A written explanation of the budget would accompany it in a proposal.

Double-check your math. I once heard an experienced foundation program officer say that one-third of the proposals she reviews have math errors. Those errors subtract from the confidence placed in a proposal, and create a difference between the amount you need and the amount you requested.

When there are math errors in a proposal, the message being sent to a potential grant maker is: "Trust us with a lot of your money. We are highly competent people. We just can't add or subtract real well."

Discussing **funding for the future** is a highly significant part of the cost section. *Grant makers will definitely want to know what happens after the grant money runs out.* How will you continue the benefits the grant achieves? If yours is a one-time project, then there is no problem. If it is intended to be an on-going program, then where will necessary funds come from in the future? Will the grant maker be expected to provide more money? Will the program have to be dismantled? Without a good explanation your proposal will be viewed as weaker.

Grant Budget Example

	Requested:	Our Contribution or Other Sources:
Salaries and wages		
Project director $3,000 per mt. x 12 mts.	$36,000	
Benefits and taxes		
Health insurance, retirement, Social Security, etc.	7,120	
Consultants and outside services		
Dr. Karen Jones, consultant	931	
Office expenses		
(Seven percent of our building)		
144 sq. ft. at $216 per mt. x 12 mts.		$2,592
Telephone at $20 per mt. x 12 mts.		240
Utilities at $30 per mt. x 12 mts.		360
Facility insurance, prorated at $171 per yr.		171
Equipment		
Computer and printer purchase	1,857	
Office furniture purchase	2,415	
Supplies		
Office supplies per yr. (our project share)	120	
Photocopying per yr. (our project share)	190	
Travel		
Staff auto at .30 per mile x 800 miles x 12 mts.	2,880	
Other costs		
Conference: professional association meeting	475	
Postage per yr.	360	
Indirect costs		
Nine percent of requested costs above ($52,348) to pay for the administrative, accounting, clerical, and building maintenance services necessary for the operation of the grant project	4,711	
Totals	$57,059	$3,363

> A strong proposal will always show that there is a plan for the future. To say that your program will always be dependent on grants means the future may not be secure.

Generally, foundations and corporations do not make one grant after another to the same organization. They do not want to lock themselves into supporting the same few programs. They do not want to foster dependency. They want to be able to make grants for new projects. On the other hand, government grants may go on indefinitely.

Repeated grants for the same project over a few years is a type of funding called "continuation funding," "continuing support," or "renewal funding." Research will tell you whether to expect that atypical type of support from a grant maker.

APPENDIX

Lastly, add an appendix with materials that support your request. Normally included are **five items**:

- verification of your tax exempt status,
- the names of your board of trustees,
- audited financial statements,
- a summary of your organization's current annual budget,
- your annual report, if you produce one.

To verify your tax exempt status use the I.R.S. letter your organization received when the organization was formed. If you do not have your tax exemption letter from the I.R.S. write them for a letter confirming your exempt status.

Check to see what the funder wants in the appendix. This is the proposal area where the biggest differences in what funders want are seen. When in doubt send all five items. Don't miss a grant because something was left out.

Add to your table of contents page a list of the appendix contents. That will make it more clear what is in the proposal.

Some grant makers may ask questions about your board of trustees. Grant makers want to know that a board is strong, involved, and knowledgeable.

To make your request more compelling, *you might attach letters of support* from community leaders, elected officials, people whom you have helped, professionals in your field, or others who make your case stronger. The letters demonstrate interest in your proposal and validate what it says. Community support is often highly valued, especially by government grant makers. If you choose to use letters of support, don't put in more than about two or three letters. That's enough to get the point across. You might provide guidance to the persons drafting the letters, such as to concentrate on some aspect of your organizational effectiveness, or on the need for the grant. Have the letters of support sent to you. That way you will know what the letters say, and that they were done. You could even use copies of the letters about this proposal if you have to write to more than one funder.

It's your proposal and you are free to add anything that will clarify the request or influence the grant maker. *Materials about your organization* such as a brochure or background information may be added to the appendix. When there are resumes, job descriptions, studies, technical specifications, diagrams, price quotations, or other documents, the appendix is the place for them. In addition, you might attach data on your benefits to past clients, copies of evaluations your organization has gotten, letters that have recognized the effectiveness of your operation, or copies of accreditations and awards received. Consider using visual materials when a picture is worth a thousand words. The items in the appendix may not be closely read so put key facts into the previous sections of the proposal also.

Include documentation in the appendix of the cost of any very expensive purchases, such as a piece of equipment running several thousand dollars. Wages can be a large cost, but you don't normally need to supply documentation of the wages to be paid, unless there is an expensive contract for services.

PROPOSAL TIPS

We have now looked at the eight parts of a standard grant proposal. Remember to **use any forms funders require**, and to follow any *procedures* they require. Don't return blank forms, or leave question raising blank spaces, especially for government grants. Write in "not applicable" where appropriate.

Ask questions when you are unclear about what the funder expects of you. That is always a good idea.

If you are not seeking funds for a special project, but instead want general *operating support*, follow the same basic eight step proposal format. Discuss the overall organization, its needs, goals, benefits, and plans. Instead of a specific evaluation, indicate past successes and on-going general evaluation results. Instead of a project budget, summarize your organizational budget situation. The proposal format is the same, just expand it to the whole of your operations.

A grant seeker once told me that she heard the key to getting a grant is the writing style used. I disagree with that idea. Good writing is helpful, however the substance, what the grant will do, is more important than the writing style.

> Use the grant proposal work sheet at the end of the chapter to help you get started in preparing your first proposal draft. Make it work for you. The work sheet poses questions which a funder would ask. By answering these questions you will construct a grant proposal line by line.

After you have the basics on paper you can refine the ideas and the wording. Professional writers say that **editing is essential** in good writing. Read the tentative proposal copy on several days, and edit it each day. The proposal will get better each time.

Don't try to impress a funder with an expensively printed proposal that looks extravagant, as though you've got money to burn. Staple the proposal together, don't bind it. Often it will be taken apart anyway, to photocopy for distribution.

Your proposal does not have to be a great work of art. There are *no* Pulitzer Prizes for grant proposals. The proposal will *not* end up in the Smithsonian Museum. The persons who make grants do understand that you are not an expert at grant proposal writing. Your expertise is appropriately in another area. If you do not get things exactly right, well, funders are used to that. Whatever you submit, they will have seen worse! This takes some pressure off you. You will not be held to a standard of perfection. Because you are reading this book you are going to be ahead of other grant seekers who have not bothered to learn about the grants process.

While the proposal does not have to be perfect, it ought to be a decent piece of work. The proposal should, of course, be neatly typed and checked for spelling or grammar errors. One grammar error which is much in vogue at present, is to use "their" (a plural word) when referring to one person. As in, "A person should proofread their proposal." *One* person cannot proofread *their* own proposal. "His" is the traditional word to use when the gender could be either male or female. As alternatives, you may say: A person should proofread her proposal. A person should proofread his or her proposal. A person should proofread a proposal. They should proofread their proposal. Proofread the blasted proposal! But you may not say, a person should proofread their proposal… unless that individual has a multiple personality.

> It is very important to *always have someone inside and someone outside your nonprofit proofread the grant request.* Errors, unclear statements, or weaknesses may be spotted that you would never have noticed.

Where do you think a grantor is going to say the proposal is weak? Go back and add explanations and justifications.

The proposal may well be the only example of your work a funder sees. Thus a funder's judgment about your organization's ability to do quality work is based in part on your proposal. The proposal should reflect well on you. There is a subconscious tendency to assume that a sharp looking, carefully prepared proposal is evidence of competence and a careful thinking. I have seen proposals whose appearance indicated that someone put a lot of work into them. I was impressed by that.

Hiring a grants consultant is not necessary and not usually done. But it is an option. To find fund-raising professionals obtain referrals from people or organizations you know such as the United Way, check the yellow pages, check fund-raising magazine ads, or contact the Association of Fundraising Professionals, which prepares a consultants guide. The A.F.P. national office is at: Suite 700, 1101 King St., Alexandria, VA 22314. Their phone number is 1 (800) 666-FUND. Some libraries have directories of available consultants, such as *Consultants & Consulting Organizations Directory.* There is a web site about grants consultants: http://www.lib.msu.edu/harris23/grants/fraisers.htm.

If you hire a grants consultant, you will still have to tell that person what to write. He or she won't know anything about what you want to do, or about your organization. So a consultant cannot attempt to get a grant for you without your complete involvement. No consultant can, or will guarantee that you will get a grant.

The norm is not to ask for reimbursement for a proposal writer through the grant. This is an expense that should be absorbed by a nonprofit.

A *deadline* may need to be met if you want the funds by a certain time. The funder might make grants each month, or possibly four times a year. Some funding sources could take months to reply to your proposal. The check will arrive even later. If the funder awards grants only twice a year, you have to adjust your timing accordingly. You might wish to mail the proposal when it won't just sit, waiting for the next decision making meeting. Try to send the proposal at least four weeks before the deadline. That way there is time for the funder to ask for additional information if something else is needed. Mail the number of copies of the proposal requested.

After sending the proposal, you ought to **follow up after about two weeks**, if no response has been received. You should contact the potential funding source, not expecting a decision, but to see that the proposal has been received, to answer any questions they have, to ask questions you have about their grant making process, and to request an appointment to discuss the proposal.

At times, grant makers may want to visit your organization and see its operations. If so, the site visit demonstrates their interest, and can be a fine opportunity to make a good impression. For a site visit, find out what the representative of the funder wants to see, add what you want him to see, and develop an agenda. Provide copies of written materials that support the grant request for the person visiting your facility to examine later.

When hosting or visiting a grant maker, your chief executive officer, the president of your board, and another person who is knowledgeable about the grant proposal should participate. Prepare a list of the major points you want to get across at the meeting.

Fewer than 10% of foundations, just the largest ones, have an office of their own. So for you to visit a foundation may not be possible.

> There is *a lot of variation* in the interaction you can expect with grant makers after sending a proposal. Some grant makers have no communication with grant applicants after receiving the grant request. One funder says the only communication is: "If your request is denied, you get a note. If your request is approved, you get a check." On the other end of the spectrum, one foundation employee says their staff will ask you a lot of questions before a decision is made.

Your request for a grant most often will be evaluated by a group, such as the distribution committee of a foundation. Corporations rely on a few executives to make the decisions. Larger funders and the government use their staff in the decision making process.

There might be a little negotiation about the grant and how it will be used. You may be asked to modify your plan, accept a lower dollar total, or take partial funding and get the rest from other donors. When you are offered a grant you can respond with: "yes," "no," or "maybe." If you get fundamentally what you want, you say "yes." If there are serious complications, though that very seldom happens, you might want to say "no," and proceed to other potential funders. If you are offered some conditions you do not like, then you say "maybe" and negotiate. You might want to lower your goals if you are offered less money than you originally sought. Doing this will help during the evaluation of goal achievement. If the grant amount is only part of what you really need, you should accept the grant, and seek another funder to support the program also. The government is more likely than foundations or corporations to try to negotiate downward the grant amount you requested.

With a grant above $100,000 there is more often budget negotiation. Large grants are more complicated in other aspects too, as you would expect. In most cases, with all types of funders, you will get the amount you requested.

Grant seeking is a competitive process. More money is requested than is available. If you are turned down, *find out why*. Ask if it was due to the presentation, the content, or whether they just had on hand what were perceived as stronger proposals. Perhaps there was a misunderstanding, or there are *modifications which will make the request successful*. If the answer is really a definite no, don't push, accept it with grace. Knowing what the funder did not like is useful, because you will want to consider changes before you send the request to the next funding source on your prospect list, a more insightful funder.

You can't win 'em all. That's what they say, and they are right. Perhaps you sent out four different proposals for $25,000 each. Things did not go well, and only two were funded. You are still $50,000 ahead of where you would have been! So it is worthwhile to keep trying.

Unfortunately, some funders will never respond at all. After a few follow up letters or phone calls with no replies, you must move on to another funding source. It is irresponsible, but a few smaller funders will reject proposals by tossing them in the wastebasket and doing nothing else.

When you do receive a grant, you may be asked to sign a contract. In effect, you are making a contract about the use of the grant anyway. You have already stated in writing exactly how the grant money will be used. For a grant recipient to spend money from a grantor for something other than the purposes in the proposal is wrong. That misuse creates ethical, credibility, and legal problems. Check with the funder before making significant modifications to the plan or budget because that alters the grant agreement.

Don't spend money based on a "verbal understanding." Wait for the written acknowledgment or the check. With some government grants, payment will be made after the expenses occur, as reimbursement. Also, you ought to note if the funds must be expended by a certain date.

Some funders will send written "terms of the grant" or a grant award letter, a letter officially authorizing the grant. The terms of the grant will include a statement of the responsibilities of the grantor and your organization as the grantee. The funder might set up reporting requirements. There might be an audit if the grant is a very large amount. But that usually only happens with government grants. You will be informed of these expectations when getting the grant. Make sure you understand what the funder expects of you.

> After hearing you will get a grant, write down on your calendar the schedule of follow up activities and reports due. If you do not want to handle the follow up, appoint someone in your organization to be responsible for compliance with the grant requirements.

Establish financial and other record keeping systems for the grant. Create a separate account for the grant expenses, so you can easily know what was spent. Save all the records and receipts. Have your accountant set things up for you. Your organization can follow basically the same financial practices it always does.

Make an entry on your calendar also to report back to the funding source on the total grant project expenditures. That could go with your evaluation report to them. If you have money left over from the grant project, take the initiative to contact the grant maker with your ideas about how to handle that. Maybe you can expand the grant program. The grant money was sent for only one purpose and cannot be used for something else unless authorized by the grant maker.

If you need more money, it just might be possible that the grant maker will provide extra funds to pay for added expenses above the original grant. To make a request for more funding probably will lower the funder's opinion of your work, depending on the reasons for the cost overrun. So offer good reasons for needing more money.

Reinforcement of donor behavior is important for future grant seeking. A personal *thank you letter* to the grant maker is standard practice. I've heard of a case where a principal receiving a grant for her small school had some of the students handwrite construction paper thank you notes. The foundation trustees have still not forgotten that. An extra effort like that is not required. But if you can think of a special little way to make the thank you more memorable, that would be a nice touch.

GOVERNMENT GRANT PROPOSALS

Lastly, we shall look briefly at government grants. Sometimes a foundation or corporation will ask you to fill out application forms they provide. With a government grant that is usually the case. Make copies of the original forms and use the copies for the first draft and revisions.

> Often a completed Standard Form 424 is required to request federal funds. Included in a federal grant application may be their budget forms, plus legal certifications and assurances that you will be informed of. The certifications and assurances may be about such matters as: having a drug free workplace, non-discrimination, having had no serious federal grant problems in the past, and compliance with various federal laws.

With a government grant you may be allowed to attach letters of support or supporting documents. You should check into this possibility because those items can add strength to your request.

You might be allowed to receive copies of previously successful government grant applications because they are public records. Ask the grant making agency about this since the information will be quite useful to you. Some bureaucrats are reluctant to send previous proposals even though (in most situations) these proposals are by law supposed to be available for public review.

> At times with a government grant you will be asked to provide a "narrative" (a detailed written description) stating your grant request, or you will be given no specific direction as to the format for writing your proposal. When no format is specified, use the eight step proposal format described in this chapter.

Government agencies may require a pre-application proposal. That is used to make sure the proposal is on the right track, and to weed out some applications before final proposals are submitted.

Ask about the **rating system** that will be used in evaluating your grant request. Government agencies often use formal rating procedures, sometimes giving points for the strong aspects of each proposal. For the key parts of a government grant, especially those which are awarded evaluation points, go into detail. Don't lose any points by not addressing all the topics for which points are given.

For competitive grants an often decisive factor in being successful is how strong the nonprofit organization is. Place emphasis on proving that yours is an effective organization which can do great work. Show that your nonprofit has a fine track record, good staff, lots of expertise, and the resources to do the job.

Often a team of experts, some in government and some not, will read and rate your proposal. Always request a copy of the comments made by those who have rated your government grant application.

Some federal grant applications must be reviewed at the state level. Your state's "single point of contact" will do that. The *Catalog of Federal Domestic Assistance* will indicate if there is such a requirement. About half the states have chosen to participate in this process. The single point of contact process (if it exists in your state) allows for local review and comment, plus better coordination of federal grant activity. A federal agency's application package should also have instructions about this review, which is also known as "Executive Order 12372 review." There is a list in the *Catalog of Federal Domestic Assistance* of the state contacts. Those persons can be of aid to you in understanding how this aspect of the federal grant system works.

Very similar to grants are "cooperative agreements." Your organization and the government would interact as a team to carry out a plan. So the cooperative agreement is more than a transfer of money, it is working together.

> Getting **state and local grants** is similar to getting federal grants. You can learn their specific procedures by contacting the department administrator in charge of making the grant you want. Each specific government agency can use its own unique forms, application process, and method of decision making. A government agency may also have its own rules for administering grants once they are made.

Government agencies have strict rules. One reason government agencies do not allow exceptions to their rules is that they would be open to accusations of favoritism or to legal trouble if they did. A protest could come from some competing organizations which did follow the rules, but were turned down.

Federal grants are rigid when it comes to the deadlines. There is no such thing as a late proposal.

When you get a government grant for your nonprofit, be sure you understand the rules for financial management of the grant funds. Start by asking the government employee you have been dealing with to give you a complete list of the requirements. Federal Office of Management and Budget circulars will also give you guidance on federal financial and accounting matters.

Consider the following questions which could affect your organization after receiving a government grant. Must you set up a special account and deposit the grant in it? What rules affect your spending the money? What reports are required?

Government auditors who might review your grant program tend to focus on whether: the record keeping was accurate, expenditures were for an allowable purpose, your matching funds were given, the grant plan was followed, and program participants were eligible.

When you are asked to match part of the grant with your own organizational contribution, remember to consider your indirect costs as a possibility. The time of volunteers might also be considered as a matching contribution in some cases. Assign a reasonable per hour valuation for the volunteer labor.

Government grants may require "maintenance of effort." If so, recipients may not reduce their own existing funding effort for a program, and then substitute federal dollars to make up the difference.

For more information on federal grants, see a book specializing in federal grants such as *Finding Funding: Grantwriting and Project Management From Start to Finish* by Brewer, Achilles, and Fuhriman. In addition the *Catalog of Federal Domestic Assistance* has information about the federal grants process.

CLOSING THOUGHTS

One ingredient in the recipe for good writing is to add shortening. So I am going to conclude here with a few closing thoughts.

Make use of the proposal work sheet (which follows) to help you get started writing a proposal. This work sheet is a way of dealing with writer's block, a blank white sheet of paper staring you in the face and you don't know what to write. The work sheet summarizes the content of a complete and effective proposal. To finish the work sheet is to have written a grant proposal. Use this step by step guide to begin your proposal. The work sheet can also be used to test a finished proposal. If your proposal does not answer all the questions, something may be missing.

Following the proposal worksheet is a sample grant proposal written a few years ago. The appendix materials from the proposal have not been included to save your time. However, the table of contents lists what was in the appendix. The organization requesting this foundation grant is trying to build its endowment. An endowment is a permanent reserve fund of assets held for the security and income the endowment provides.

Your proposal could employ the style and format of this sample proposal. Of course, the content of any proposal is the most important aspect.

Some persons are stopped at the point of proposal writing because they are hesitant to begin. The way to begin is to *plunge right in*. There is money waiting. You really can get a grant!

GRANT PROPOSAL WORK SHEET

To begin a grant proposal, answer the questions below. These are questions a funder might ask. The answers can be the *first draft* of your request for a grant. Add any other information that is significant. Even in a short proposal, you ought to write two or three paragraphs for each of the first seven sections. Edit the proposal to make it read smoothly.

Summary

- What is your organization requesting a grant to do?
- What is the need?
- What are the goals of the grant?
- Who will benefit from this grant and how?
- What plan will you use to achieve the goals and benefits?
- How much is the total cost of the plan, and what grant amount is requested?

Our Organization

- What are the mission and activities of your organization?
- Whom do you help, and where are they located?
- How would you describe your organization?
- What should the funder know which will build confidence about your nonprofit?
- What are some organizational accomplishments?
- What are the qualifications of the staff who will manage the grant program?

Need

- What is the need the grant will address?
- Who has the need?
- How bad is the situation?

- What are the consequences of the unmet need?
- What evidence proves this need exists?

Goals and Benefits

- Would you state grant goals that are measurable and numerical?
- What ultimate benefits will occur because the goals were reached?
- How many people will the grant benefit?
- Where are the locations which will be affected by the grant?

Plan

- How exactly will you achieve the goals and benefits?
- What is the time frame, who will do what and when?
- What staffing and major purchases are necessary to reach the goals and benefits?
- Why will the plan be effective?
- Why will the plan be efficient?

Evaluation

- How will you determine the degree of success in attaining the goals and benefits?
- Who is going to measure what… how and when?
- In what way can your results be measured statistically?

Cost

- What expenditures are necessary to carry out the plan?
- Have you written an explanation of the expenses, and also added a budget like the budget example?
- What is your organization contributing to pay for the plan?

- What are the projected sources of income, including other grants, for the grant project?
- How will you continue the benefits the grant achieves after the grant funds run out?

Appendix

- Have you included the appropriate items from the description of the appendix?

★ WASHINGTON COUNTY ARTS CENTER ★

2500 Anderson Blvd.
Franklin, Ohio 44356
(614) 952-3717

April 26, 1999

Mrs. Danielle Adams
Stephen Ray Foundation
277 N. Wheatland Ave.
Franklin, Ohio 44357

Dear Mrs. Adams:

We are requesting a grant from your foundation to employ a consultant to establish a fund-raising plan for our Arts Center. This comprehensive fund-raising plan will build our financial resources to create a better future for our organization and the people we serve. We have selected an experienced fund-raising consultant to set up the plan. This new plan will include highly productive revenue generating methods, such as planned giving programs and major gift solicitations. The target for the plan is to raise $450,000. This money will be used for building our organization's endowment. The proposal with this letter describes our program in detail.

This grant will make possible a dramatic advance for the Arts Center. The ultimate beneficiaries from a financially stronger Arts Center will be the present and future citizens of our county. We call this initiative, "A Legacy For The Future." The Arts Center is especially important in this rural county because we provide unique cultural, recreational, and educational advantages. We make art, music, theater, and dance come alive for many citizens.

The grant amount we are requesting from your foundation is $29,000 for the development of the fund-raising plan and consulting services. This investment will allow the Arts Center to realize substantial benefits. Your foundation has a tradition of valuable support for the arts. Consideration of our proposal will be appreciated. I will be glad to answer any questions you have about our grant request. If your schedule permits, I would like to have a meeting with you to personally discuss this proposal.

Sincerely,

Debbie Bassett

Debbie Bassett
President of the Board
Washington County Arts Center

DB/ga
enclosure

WASHINGTON COUNTY ARTS CENTER
2500 Anderson Blvd. Franklin, Ohio 44356 (614) 952-3717

"A Legacy For The Future"

Grant Proposal
Submitted to the Stephen Ray Foundation
April 26, 1999

TABLE OF CONTENTS

Summary   Page 1
Our Organization   1
Need   2
Goals & Benefits   2
Plan   3
Evaluation   4
Cost   4
Appendix: 6
Letter of support from the Ohio Arts Council   6
Letter of support from the county commissioners   7
Editorial in *The Washington Herald*   8
Names of our board of trustees   9
I.R.S. letter showing our tax exemption   10
Audited financial statements   11
Our current budget   16
Resume of the consultant   17
Contract to be offered to the consultant   18
Our annual report   20

A LEGACY FOR THE FUTURE

SUMMARY:

We are requesting a grant to develop a **comprehensive fund-raising plan** for the Washington County Arts Center. During its eleven year history, the Arts Center has not had a complete plan that would advance its financial situation. Occasional fund-raising has been done, however the results were not as good as if professional help had been used. We have a total endowment of only $21,739. Most arts facilities depend on endowment funds and gifts for a significant percentage of their income.

Our board of trustees has concluded that the long-term health of the Arts Center requires a complete and professionally guided fund-raising master plan. This written three-year plan will include as components: a capital campaign, major gifts, planned giving, annual giving, and special events. Our goal is to make the Arts Center financially stronger so that its benefits to our community will grow. The benefits from the fund-raising plan will extend long into the future.

The Arts Center is a high profile institution which meets the cultural needs of this county through concerts, plays, art exhibitions, and dance performances. Our motto is, "Making the arts come alive in your life."

The grant we are requesting will create an exciting opportunity to hire Dr. Bob Lappin, an experienced financial consultant. He will prepare a detailed comprehensive fund-raising plan for the Arts Center, and coach us in carrying it out. Based on our initial discussions with him, we intend to raise $450,000 for our endowment in the three years of the plan. The consultant's fee is $29,000, and thus we are asking for a grant in that amount from your foundation. The cost section of this proposal shows the other expenses to implement our program, and the other sources of financial support. The David R. Sanor Foundation has already made a $10,000 grant to pay for part of the operating expenses of the plan.

OUR ORGANIZATION:

The Washington County Arts Center's mission is to present and teach music, theater, dance, and visual arts, and to serve as a vital resource meeting the cultural needs of Washington County citizens. Our organization is located in Franklin, Ohio. There is a countywide population of about 170,000 persons. The Arts Center is a tax-exempt 501(c)(3) organization.

Our colonial brick building houses an auditorium, a dance rehearsal room, two classrooms, an art gallery, and an administrative office. The building is accessible to the handicapped. There are two staff members (a director and a secretary), both full-time.

Several arts organizations officially make the Arts Center their home and are represented on the board of trustees. The organizations are a concert band, community symphony orchestra, youth dance company, theater guild, young players theater company, an art association, plus an arts and crafts club. The combined membership in these groups is 314 members. Each of these affiliated groups has its own budget. The Arts Center receives some compensation from these groups. For the Arts Center itself, the total current annual operating expenses are $186,000.

The arts facility itself is a community resource. It was used at a nominal charge for numerous meetings last year by various local organizations.

The Arts Center is an active organization. As evidence of public interest, attendance at Arts Center presentations during the last calendar year totaled 12,742 persons. A variety of different classes about the arts were offered last year. Presented by Arts Center based groups in the last year were: eleven plays, eight concerts, five dance recitals, and nine visual art exhibits. A grant from the Ohio Arts Council brought us artist-in-residence, Penny Bailey (director) for our youth theater company. Several performances were given by a professional theater company last summer. A Black History Month jazz concert was held. The annual concert by the Cincinnati Chamber Orchestra was a special event of the Christmas season.

The results of our work have been recognized in numerous ways. An editorial last year in *The Washington Herald* called the Arts Center "...a gem in this county which shines brighter every year." The editorial singled out the opportunities for persons of <u>all ages</u> as one of the best features of the Arts Center. The director of the Arts Center, Aaron Nelson, was recently given a Governor's Award for community service, based on his work at the Arts Center. The Franklin School Board recently passed a resolution recognizing the Arts Center as, "a unique and valuable asset which adds quality to the educational process."

Given that there are no large cities in the surrounding counties, the Arts Center is a *unique* organization whose special services are not otherwise available to the people of this region.

NEED:

It is important to expand our income base by developing a fund-raising program. Many arts organizations have cultivated a substantial range of funding sources. We do not have a long history (sixteen years) and our potential sources of income are largely undeveloped. We should have a planned giving program, and the only capital campaign was eleven years ago to construct our building.

The programs which the Arts Center can offer the public are related to our income. New artistic directions depend on sufficient funding to support them. With strategic income development, the Arts Center can advance. Our revenue generating efforts need to take on a more long-term focus. We want to use the most productive fund-raising techniques to take advantage of opportunities. Other arts organizations are benefiting from income sources we should use.

Because our total budget is already committed to existing programs, we are unable to fully finance the new fund-raising program. A grant would make this new program possible.

The board of trustees recognizes that the Arts Center can make significant progress through an effective plan for financial development. To improve upon the present situation will *increase our ability to achieve our mission of serving the cultural needs of the public.*

New funding will increase our modest organizational endowment. More endowment income will allow certain important changes, such as new sound equipment in the auditorium, and new lighting in the art gallery. Visitors to the Arts Center have commented on these shortcomings. Our board has recognized that on-going improvements at the Arts Center must be made.

GOALS AND BENEFITS:

Our goal is a stronger and expanded financial foundation for the Arts Center. In that way we can address the financial need identified above, and thus better serve the public in the future. We propose to prepare and follow a comprehensive multi-year plan for fund-raising. This will help us realize our potential.

This grant provides "leverage." With a comparatively small investment from your foundation, we can produce very large results. This is an efficient use of the grant funds. Once we start on this fund-raising path, we will continue beyond the first three years and realize benefits for many years into the future. Planned gifts, for example, will come to us at various times after the initial three years, yet could be based on our original work to bring in gift pledges.

To attain our goal will mean substantial benefits in both the short-term and the long-term. It is clear that a solid financial base will make the Arts Center more secure for the future. A larger endowment will earn more interest income for us. Effective fund-raising will permit us to offer more programs and classes for the Washington County community. Our three year funding target is to raise a total of $450,000.

Our benefits go to a cross-section of the people of this county. The individuals of our region are the real beneficiaries of this grant. The arts can enlarge a person's spirit. Our community is enriched because of the Arts Center.

Both the persons who attend and those who create the arts events derive significant benefits. The students who train at the Arts Center and the students who attend the cultural events have personal and educational experiences which shape their lives. Many adults find our presence in this largely rural county offers them cultural opportunities which they would never have otherwise.

A local teacher, Becky Canterbury, said: "At the Arts Center I got my first taste of the stage. That experience resulted in my majoring in speech and drama at college. As a high school teacher now, I encourage my students to use the Arts Center to develop their talents. It changed my life and it can change theirs."

Fund-raising is a tool to help us achieve our mission. This is a key point in the progress of the Arts Center, and what the Arts Center means to Washington County residents. What we do now will benefit generations to come by leaving a permanent legacy for the future.

PLAN:

Once the grant is received, we can sign a contract with Dr. Bob Lappin for his research, advice, and development of a written comprehensive fund-raising plan. Specialists associated with Dr. Lappin will assist him on some parts of the plan. Preparations will take five months from the receipt of the grant. The fund-raising plan will then be implemented over the next three years.

Because the master plan will be based on professional experience and be designed specifically for our needs, we believe it will be effective and efficient. The methods to cultivate donors have consistently worked for other nonprofit organizations. There is much room to expand upon our prior efforts and the potential is high. Of the last five organizations Dr. Lappin assisted, all of them reached their total dollar goal. Dr. Lappin will complete a feasibility study for us to give direction to the capital campaign. His resume is in the appendix. Our plan will be based on the following methods.

The capital campaign is the central part of the effort to meet our $450,000 goal. It is designed to raise a large amount of money over an extended time. The consultant will assist us in preparing an action timetable, choosing methods, identifying donors, and making our best case to them. Major gifts are a substantial part of the capital campaign. We are compiling a list of persons who might provide large monetary gifts to the Arts Center. A few financial commitments have been made already.

The planned giving component is untapped at present. Many of the patrons of our programs, the volunteers, and the participants in the Arts Center's arts organizations are capable of making large planned gifts to the Arts Center. We want to offer them information about donating assets through wills, life insurance, charitable trusts, and annuities. In some cases this can provide us with substantial income right now, not just long-term income. We will show supporters how to get tax advantages and maximize the benefits to themselves by planning their giving.

Annual giving is a yearly program we presently employ, but it will be expanded. We know that results from institutions similar to ours demonstrate that great potential exists for us. By increasing the number of givers, we will also increase the donor pool from which we could receive major gifts or planned gifts. Direct mail and telephone calls will be part of this fund-raising method.

Four special events will be scheduled to attract people to the Arts Center, and generate publicity. As an arts institution we are in a good position to offer concerts, exhibits, and performances of various types. These events will kick off the capital campaign, draw people to the Arts Center, and raise money.

No new paid staff at the Arts Center are required to administer the plan. Volunteers, the board of trustees, and existing staff will provide the manpower. The arts groups that have representatives on the Arts Center's board of trustees have agreed to provide the necessary volunteers to carry out the plan. These groups will be consulted about the final plan. Mr. Nelson, our director, will have the responsibility to manage the fund-raising effort, with the assistance of the Arts Center board, and Dr. Lappin. Three years of consulting and training services are provided for in the $29,000 fee to Dr. Lappin.

A specific schedule for the fund-raising activities will be part of the consultant's plan. We know that the major gift component will be the one we start with. The capital campaign can be announced once enough major gifts have been secured. Activity in the other components will begin within two months of the time the consultant's plan is accepted.

Our organization will issue a press release about your grant after the grant is received. That will be a part of the publicity surrounding our fund-raising effort.

EVALUATION:

Our board of trustees will evaluate the success of the fund-raising plan twice a year. They will analyze several basic issues:

1. Was the monetary goal for the period reached?
2. Is the plan being implemented well?
3. Are contributors giving us positive feedback?
4. Is a solid basis for the long-term financial health of the Arts Center being established?

A written survey of 20% of the potential donors who were contacted will be conducted after the initial six months of implementation to gather data about their reactions, and to evaluate the effectiveness of our fund-raising techniques. The Arts Center director will conduct the survey, and report to the board. He will also monitor the on-going costs of the fund-raising plan. The director will bring to the attention of the board feedback from contributors, and any significant problems in carrying out the plan.

The consultant will analyze our results and provide regular advice about how to improve our efforts. He is also to submit a report about our progress at six month intervals. That report will include a statistical analysis of who is contributing, and state how our results compare with what was projected.

The board of trustees will take the responsibility to interpret the available information. They will make an evaluation every six months during the operation of the plan, after getting the consultant's reports. The board will focus on the above four questions and numerically track the progress toward our monetary goal. The evaluations by the board are to be printed with the minutes of their meetings. A final evaluation will be prepared by the board to summarize what the outcomes were, why they occurred, and what we have learned for future use. This evaluation will be sent to your foundation.

COST:

The costs of the fund-raising program fall into several categories. These costs are necessary to achieve our goal of a financially stronger Arts Center.

There is a contract with Dr. Lappin for his and his associates' professional services. The total contract is for $29,000.

There are **expenses to conduct the three-year plan.** These include management, printing, postage, automobile mileage, long distance telephone service, gifts for donors, and special event expenses. These expenses are to be partially paid for by a $10,000 grant already made by the David R. Sanor Foundation. In addition, there are legal services necessary for establishing the planned giving programs. A commitment from a local law firm (Neff, Hill & Moore) to provide the services at no charge has been secured. These contributed legal services would otherwise cost us $6,300.

Indirect costs to carry out this program occur. These costs are the portion of our operating expenses that apply to the grant funded program. Without these indirect costs the program could not take place. We understand that it is not the policy of your foundation to reimburse indirect costs. We have not shown our indirect costs in the budget. These indirect expenses (to be paid by the Arts Center) include providing clerical support services, office space, office equipment, and office supplies.

There will be continuing <u>funding in the future</u> for this high priority fund-raising program. Expenses after the first three years will be relatively small and will be absorbed by the Arts Center. Our board of trustees is committed to continuing the program indefinitely.

The money received for our endowment from fund-raising will be invested in local bank certificates of deposit, and an index mutual fund designed to match the stock market return. The budget includes all three years of the grant program. The grant we are requesting from your foundation is $29,000.

PROGRAM BUDGET

	Requested:	Our Contribution or Other Sources:
Consultant (to develop the fund-raising plan)	$29,000	
Management of program (5% of center director's time)		$6,751
Printing (for annual & capital campaign literature)		2,743
Postage ($750 per yr. for letters and brochures)		2,250
Automobile mileage (for center director, $.25 x 7,500 miles)		1,875
Telephone service (long distance rate calls for fund-raising)		950
Gifts for donors (marble paperweights for major donors)		718
Special event expenses, four events (food, decorations, and supplies for events)		2,400
Legal services of Neff, Hill & Moore (setting up planned giving opportunities)		6,300
Totals	$29,000	$23,987

Chapter 5

CONCLUSION

**"You may be disappointed if you fail,
but you are doomed if you don't try."
Beverly Sills**

Well, it's time to wrap things up. A college student once asked his speech professor, "How many points should a good speech have?" The professor thought hard for a while and replied, "At least one." If I made at least one point in this book, I hope it was that you can get a grant.

As you think about grants, you may hear a little voice whispering inside you, saying such negative things as:

- "I can't do this." In fact, you have more than enough ability to do this. You are able to do it if you want to. It is possible.
- "I don't have the confidence it takes." Lots of people with little confidence get grant checks in the mail.
- "I don't know how to start." Getting a grant is not some deeply mysterious journey into the unknown. Just go step by step. Use the grant checklist, and the work sheets for finding a funder and writing a grant proposal. They will lead you all the way through.
- "I don't have the time." Developing your idea for the grant will take some thought. Research to find a funder could take a few hours. Writing the first draft of a simple proposal could take an afternoon. Say you invest 12 hours to get a $12,000 grant. That is a return of $1,000 per hour of your time. Not bad. Not bad at all.

There are persons who can help you at various points in the grants process. Think about asking:

- the potential funding source, for information,
- co-workers who have grants experience,
- nonprofits that have gotten grants,
- a librarian in the grants section of the library,
- the management of your nonprofit,
- your board of trustees,
- your accountant,
- a college professor, for evaluation of your program,
- a consultant,
- government officials, for letters of support and information,
- a friend, to proofread your proposal.

The best advice I can give you now is: don't try to cut corners. You will end up with a less than good effort. A good effort will produce good results. Don't skip over some aspect of the basic grant procedures.

As you spend hands on time with the grant research resources, the resources will become more clear. As you start writing the grant proposal, the parts will come together. You will learn a lot by doing. Going through a process also makes it stay in your memory better.

In the appendix that follows is a chapter on other fund-raising options, and there is a list of Internet grant related sites. The chapter on fund-raising is a basic introduction. Every nonprofit should have a complete fund-raising plan that takes advantage of the proven methods of bringing in donations.

I sincerely hope this book has been the benefit for you which I intended it to be. To have read to this chapter demonstrates that you are persistent, a very important quality in securing a grant. You have studied the entire process of getting a grant: how to find a funding source, research materials, and how to write the grant proposal. You have covered everything you need to know, all the fundamentals of getting grants.

Getting a grant is not as easy as 1-2-3. It's more like 2-4-8.

2 RESOURCES
4 QUESTIONS
8 PARTS

Start with **2** resources in looking for a foundation funder: *The Foundation Directory* and *The Foundation Directory Part 2*. Ask **4** questions: does a potential funder give for my subject, in my locality, in the amount I need, and for the type of support I want? Use the **8** part proposal format to write the grant request. If you understand the 2-4-8 idea, you understand the basics of how to get a grant.

Take another look at the grant checklist after Chapter 1. Mark those pages with a bookmark. **Use that summary as your guide to getting a grant.** The checklist is a list of what you need to do from start to finish. It is **the key** to getting a grant. I want to make this point strongly. The checklist contains **the most important steps** in securing a grant. You don't have to wonder, "What should I do next?" If you follow the checklist, you will be on the right path.

Begin your grant search while the grant concepts are still fresh in mind. *Put on your calendar what you should do to get started.* If you have a pen in one hand and a pulse in the other, you can get a grant!

To contact the author with questions or comments, write to:

Mark Guyer
4678 South Blvd.
Canton, Ohio 44718

OTHER FUND-RAISING OPTIONS

**"Life presents us with many opportunities.
Some of us take advantage of them, others race by afraid.
Today you have a chance to be your unique self, a chance
to give someone some space in your life, a chance to change...."
Author Unknown**

Grants are one way to raise money. There are many other fund-raising options to help your nonprofit. This section will discuss these other methods. Would you like to increase the financial resources of your organization? Would you like to move beyond the status quo? Status quo is Latin. I think it means "the mess we are in."

Recently I was driving to a distant grantsmanship workshop. Just when I got near my destination, I must have made a wrong turn because I ended up way, way out in the country someplace. I thought there was a small town nearby, where I could get my bearings, but I wasn't sure how many miles farther it was. Eventually, I saw an old farmer in bib jeans sitting in a rocking chair on his front porch. So I drove up to him, and called out, "How far do I have to drive to get into town from here?" "Well," he drawled, and thought for a moment, "about 25,000 miles in the direction you're headed."

The point of the story is not just that you're bound to meet a smart-mouthed farmer when you're lost in the country. It's also that there are big advantages to being headed in the right direction.

Does your organization have a financial plan that takes it in the right direction? **Every nonprofit organization should have a complete fund-raising plan**.

The poet Emily Dickinson once said, "I dwell in possibility...." We will look at possibilities for advancing your organization financially. If your nonprofit is not using the fund-raising methods which follow, then it is missing significant opportunities to increase income. Your nonprofit should have *the broadest possible base of financial support*. Donations from individuals are a larger percentage of income for most nonprofit organizations than grants are.

My intent is to briefly review some of the options with you. To go into detail about each fund-raising method would turn this book into a multi-volume set. This chapter does not tell you all you need to know about the fund-raising methods. It is only a basic introduction.

You might consider seeking professional assistance for large fund-raising projects, though consultants can be expensive. The Association of Fundraising Professionals has a list of consultants and conducts training classes. (Their address is in the Proposal Tips part of Chapter 4.) In addition there is the American Association of Fundraising Counsel (www.aafrc.org), 1 (800) 462-2372. As mentioned before, you can also locate consultants through recommendations, libraries, phone books, advertisements, etc.

Do it yourself fund-raising works. Study the fund-raising methods in depth. A large library will have many relevant books. You can learn what you need to know from them. Magazines such as *Contributions* will provide good money raising ideas. You may want to examine a copy and subscribe to it: *Contributions*, P.O. Box 338, Medfield MA 02052, 1 (508) 359-0019.

Fund-raising can be exciting and meaningful, not to mention quite useful. Success puts the fun in fund-raising.

> There are many persons who believe in your organization and really want to give to it. At age 87, Oseola McCarty of Mississippi gave a university scholarship fund for needy students over $170,000. She never graduated from high school, never married, never owned a car, and made her living by taking in laundry. When the pages of her Bible fell out, she taped them back in. It did not appear to her neighbors that she had any wealth. But she did manage to save some money. She gave much of her savings away, because she deeply wanted today's students to have advantages that she never had. Miss McCarty said, "I can't do everything, but I can do something to help somebody. And what I can do, I will do."

There are also people in your community who want to give. There are persons who give from the heart. Some of them will surprise you.

CULTIVATION OF DONORS

Cultivation of donors is an essential aspect of fund-raising. Cultivation involves nurturing potential and current givers by *educating and motivating* them over a period of time.

Contact supporters to inform and involve them, not just when you want money. Bring them in to meet your staff, the administration, and the group you help. Ask the supporters to volunteer, ask them for their opinions, make them feel part of your organization. As with building any relationship, it takes time. Eventually relationship building creates mutual understanding, trust, and caring.

You bring givers to the point of being vitally involved in the mission of your agency through personal contacts and regular communication by letter, phone, or meetings. When considering your nonprofit, the donor should visualize a human face, not just your letterhead stationery. The giver should not think about giving to "your" organization, but to "our" organization.

Pastor Knute Larson made a good point when he said, "People who know little about you will give little." There are steps in relationship building. Here are some ways to build up increasing involvement with donors and potential donors.

- Put them on your mailing list
- Educate them about the benefits of contributing to your organization
- Invite them to your organization's special events
- Ask for financial contributions
- Recognize all contributions made
- Evaluate the future giving potential of donors
- Offer on-going opportunities to contribute money
- Introduce them to people in the group helped
- Arrange for them to meet the organization's leadership
- Involve them in volunteer work to achieve the organization's mission
- Recruit them for committee positions

PLANNED GIVING

Planned giving is a very important way to raise money from donors. Planned giving is the donor's distribution of his or her assets by planning ahead. Reliable estimates indicate that during the next twenty years as older Americans pass away, they will bequeath over seven trillion dollars. People tend to build up assets over a lifetime. They can't take it with them. One rich Texan said, "If I can't take it with me, I just ain't gonna go." That's what he thinks.

Another man, an old miser, told his wife that he had hidden a box of cash in the attic of their house. He planned to take the money with him when he died, as his spirit ascended upward to heaven. One day his time came, and he passed away at home. Later his wife searched all through the attic and finally discovered the box. She looked inside and the cash was still there. She exclaimed, "I knew it! I told him to put the money in the basement."

Some people realistically plan for the future, others do not. Some people plan for the bequest of their assets, others do not. Some people plan well for eternity, others do not. It is smart to plan ahead.

Eighty percent of planned giving is through wills. You can start an effective planned giving program by asking to be included in wills. A substantial majority of adults, unwisely, do *not* have wills. Nonetheless, bequests of money made through wills exceed the amount of corporate giving. Deceased people actually give away even more money than corporations do.

I once heard a story about a man who believed in reincarnation. In his will he tried to leave everything to himself. Didn't work. Everything that everyone owns will be given away eventually. One method of giving is for a donor to pay for a life insurance policy with your agency as the beneficiary.

The big advantage with planned giving is that the donations can be **huge**. Instead of receiving a gift of $30, you might receive a gift of $30,000.

About 90% of an average person's wealth is in property and investment assets, while only 10% is held in cash. So it makes sense to *focus on gifts of assets*, because that's where the money is. Planned giving focuses on assets. Many of your backers will give when they are made aware of the benefits and methods of giving.

Planned giving options include a pooled income fund, in which the donor gives *assets* to a special fund and receives part of the *income* earned by that fund, for a set period of time or until death, at which time the assets are given to your charitable group. Thus the donor can met his financial needs during his lifetime, and still make a gift to your nonprofit. It is a win-win situation, just like the next options. A trust established by an individual is simpler to handle than a pooled income fund. In a **charitable remainder trust** a person sets up a trust and receives the income from the assets in the trust fund. Those assets ("the remainder") are designated to become the property of a charity after a set time. In a **charitable lead trust** the income flow is reversed. The current income from the trust assets goes to the charity *now*, and the assets go (after the life of the donor) to his heirs. A life estate management arrangement allows a donor to give a house to a nonprofit while preserving the donor's right to live in the house for life. Or a donor can give an organization assets, and in exchange receive income regularly during his lifetime through an **annuity**.

The tax code is on your side. There are enticing tax benefits for a donor who makes a planned giving contribution during life. A transfer of stock or property may allow the donor to avoid capital gains taxes plus take a major income tax deduction.

Make sure that all of your agency supporters are offered a definite opportunity to include your organization in their estate planning. Make sure they understand that there are many giving possibilities. A letter and a brochure about the advantages of planned giving can generate a substantial long-term return. Send it to all the persons connected with your nonprofit. Consider for special attention, such as following up with phone calls, those donors over 65 who have made regular gifts. Also include board members and staff.

In a group of even a hundred people, there are inevitably going to be some who are wealthy, and almost all have thousands of dollars in assets. You will be amazed at the assets of some persons who live quite modestly. One main reason those persons have substantial savings is because they do not have lavish lifestyles.

One of the clear benefits in some forms of planned giving is that it is possible for your organization to **get a large contribution now**. You do not have to wait ten or twenty years.

To establish a planned giving program, see a professional specializing in this field: an attorney or a financial consultant. Banks and trust companies can be of assistance in planned giving as sources of information and as trustees. You can handle the promotion of the giving plans once they are set up. Persons who are asked to make any large gift should always be advised in writing that they should check with their own financial or legal advisor before giving.

PLANNED GIVING EXAMPLE

Karen McKinley, a widow, had been a devoted Girl Scout leader for many years. She decided to contribute $100,000 worth of corporate stock to the local district of the Girl Scouts. The stock produced low dividends, about 2% per year ($2,000), so the current income was not very great. Mrs. McKinley made an arrangement with the development office of the Girl Scouts to give $100,000 of stock in exchange for an annuity.

The nonprofit organization benefited because it received a gift of stock which will appreciate in value over the years. The stock price had been increasing 8% a year during the last three years.

Mrs. McKinley benefited because she will receive variable annuity payments for life, payments equal to 6% of the stock value ($6,000) in the first year. So her current income went up. Mrs. McKinley avoided a large amount of capital gains taxes (about $14,000 in federal and state taxes) which she would have paid if she had sold the stock. In addition she qualified for federal income tax deductions, which will save her about $10,000 in taxes. Both the Girl Scouts and Mrs. McKinley were pleased with the transaction.

(Always check the specific situation with a tax expert before reaching conclusions about tax benefits.)

MAJOR GIFTS

Major gifts are usually secured when a relationship has been in existence for years, and a deep bond between the donor and the organization exists. The process might even be likened to a courtship. The relationship progresses to greater levels of interaction, understanding, concern, emotion, and thus commitment. As the donor shares in the life of your organization, as heart-felt commitment increases, financial commitment follows. A large gift of thousands of dollars can be the result.

Some donors will even suggest other potential givers. Donors are your willing partners. You are doing what they want done. You are giving them something of value. What kinds of benefits will the donor get from contributing? He or she may have positive feelings from belonging to a good organization, helping people in need, doing something important, receiving recognition, or leaving a personal legacy.

Listen to a potential donor. She will tell you what projects and contribution amounts she is most interested in. Concentrate on those in your communications with her.

Match the donor with an appropriate request. To get a major gift you must select the right person to ask the right donor for the right amount for the right reasons.

> Research indicates that face to face asking produces a donation generally about 50% of the time. A phone-a-thon has a much smaller success rate, and impersonal direct mail has a low percentage success rate. The more personal "the ask" the better the result.

When having a personal meeting to ask for a major gift, outline **"the case"** for the gift in advance, to prepare yourself. The case statement is the presentation of who you are, what you want to do, and the reasons people should give. The case must be motivational. It answers the question: "Why should I donate to this organization?" Some experts advise, "Let your cause do the talking."

The appeal ought to speak to both the head and the heart. Many people will give only when their feelings are moved. It has been said that the case should "...convey a feeling of importance, relevance, and urgency, and have whatever stuff is needed to warm the heart and stir the mind."

A good fund-raiser does not talk mostly about money. Instead he or she talks about how problems can be solved, and the people who will be helped. Paint a picture of how a donor can make a meaningful difference in the lives of other people. The donor is shown how giving will achieve *what the donor wants*. The giver should *take pride* in your organization's success stories, *feel the significance* of the personal needs being met, and *understand the benefits* of the work.

Think through "the close" (how you will phrase the closing request for a donation). Always ask a person for a specific amount. If a person says he will think about it, then supply information to help motivate the gift, and set a time to get back to him.

If he says "no" find out if there is an amount he would feel more comfortable giving, or why he does not want to contribute. Maybe there is a concern, or a misconception that can be dealt with.

When a person mails in a $1,000 check that sends a message: "Contact me again. I may give more." At times there is a fine line between cultivation and pestering a giver. It may take a dozen acts of kindness to win a friend, but only a single thoughtless act to lose one. You need to encourage closeness without being pushy or incessantly present.

Always say thank you for any gift. Behavior that is reinforced is repeated. Thanking the donor should be more personal and more elaborate as the gift level rises. To the standard acknowledgement, add a personal note, or a phone call, or lunch with the C.E.O. (When getting a large donation, consult the giver before you publicize it. Some people will want a major gift kept private.)

CAPITAL CAMPAIGNS

Another important option is the capital campaign. A capital campaign is an extensive fund-raising project designed to raise large amounts of capital. It is usually anchored by a few major gifts. There is inevitably a pyramid of giving with a few major donations at the top, more but smaller gifts in the middle, and numerous small gifts at the base of the pyramid. *Ten percent* of the donors often give about *sixty percent* of the total raised in a capital campaign.

Of the donors eighty percent will typically be persons who have donated to your organization previously. A gift table should be established which displays gift amounts and the anticipated number of contributions at each amount.

Leadership gifts from the board of trustees and major donors kickoff a capital campaign. The board and the C.E.O. must be committed to the campaign. Often *professional fund-raising consultants* are employed. The campaign may last one to five years.

Use the "top down, inside out" method of prospecting. This is defined as starting with givers at the highest level of donations, and with givers who are closest to the nonprofit (such as board members and volunteers). Then you approach other potential donors. If you can convince some of your top prospects to serve on the capital campaign committee, that is wonderful.

You ought to appeal to all of your past and potential contributors. On average you will need to ask four persons for each donation you want. This is because some people will say no, and some others will give less than the amount asked for.

Many colleges and universities have capital campaigns to finance construction projects, or to build their endowments. These institutions have led the way in demonstrating what can be done in fund-raising. Just one division of

Harvard University, the business school, has an endowment of well over $600 million. They probably don't start their fund-raising letters by saying: "Hi, we already have over 600 million dollars in the bank, but would you please send us more money?"

Many small colleges have tens of millions of dollars in the bank to secure a healthy future. It would be unwise not to. Cash turns a lot of ideas into reality. Most nonprofit institutions ought to have some endowment, both for the earnings and as insurance against hard times.

Can a small nonprofit really build a big endowment? Grinnell College in Iowa has about 1,400 students. The college has an endowment of more than one billion dollars. Over several decades the cumulative effect of fund-raising, saving, and investing is dramatic.

How do you start to plan a capital campaign? A **feasibility study** to test the water and develop a plan usually prepares the way for a capital campaign. A professional fund-raiser could do a feasibility study, also called a precampaign assessment. This is looking before leaping. A feasibility study is a survey of fund-raising potential that includes assessment of: the attitudes toward your organization, the motivating power of the case for funds, the ability of the constituency (your supporters) to give, and the availability of leaders and volunteers. The results lead into a planning phase. A feasibility study may cost $10,000, $20,000, or much more, depending on the situation and the scope of the campaign.

The planning should address: your objectives, your methods, who will be on the campaign committee, the case to be made to potential contributors, your timetable, identification of prospective donors, and the resources needed (volunteers, paid staff, budget) for the capital campaign. The gift table is prepared. Multi-year pledges might be advisable. Usually teams of gift solicitors will make personal contacts. Use peer to peer solicitations. To get an appointment with a company president often requires a call from your nonprofit's C.E.O. Mailings, phone calls, and other fund-raising methods figure into the plan.

There will normally be a campaign kickoff event, a campaign theme, and a victory celebration. After implementation of the campaign, a post campaign review should take place. A capital campaign may cost around 10% of the amount to be raised.

ANNUAL GIVING PROGRAMS

Annual giving programs generate once a year revenue. As usual, past donors are the best giving prospects. These are the same people who are most likely to make major gifts and participate in planned giving. People who contribute once to an annual fund drive tend to continue with yearly donations.

It is still vital, though, to do **prospect research** to keep adding people to the core group of your financial supporters. Prospect research seeks to understand a person's charitable interests and giving ability. To find prospects who may donate you could use various methods. For example, a doctor who is connected with your organization might tell you about other doctors who are potential new contributors. Your board could suggest names of their peers. Ask current donors for the names of people who might develop an interest in your organization's goals. Everyone who has contacted your nonprofit should be asked later to contribute. First you should begin the cultivation process with the prospective donors.

Foundations and corporations may also contribute. They might donate a few hundred or a few thousand dollars to an annual fund campaign.

The United Way has the best known annual giving program. You could learn from their methods. An annual giving program should have a fund-raising plan, a set dollar goal, a list of potential contributors, a campaign kickoff event, reliance on volunteer solicitors, regular progress reports, and a victory celebration. There should be a sense of excitement. Personal visits, direct mail, speaking to groups (Rotary, Elks, etc.), and phone calls can be used in conducting an annual giving program.

Organizations often use gift clubs that recognize donors based on the annual giving levels. There might be a V.I.P. Club, a Founder's Society, Gold Level Sponsors, etc. This recognition is a means to encourage participation and increased giving. There could be special perks that benefit members at each level.

An annual campaign relies heavily on direct mail and phone calls. Donations come from a donor's current income. By contrast a capital campaign relies heavily on personal meetings and donations from a donor's assets.

What if you use good fund-raising techniques and the results are poor? One reason for poor results in any fund-raising is not having energized people involved who will work hard enough to bring success. As always, motivation is a key element of success. If the volunteers are not strong in their commitment, they will not convey to possible donors a passion for your mission. Another reason for poor results is a message problem. The case statement is just not compelling enough.

An effective message showing why this particular contribution should be made is fundamental to success.

> Keep useful records. You should have a donor's gift history, interests, and correspondence. Make notes when you have a personal contact so that six months later you can surprise the donor with what a great memory you have. The donor will wonder how you recalled his hospitalization, or the new job of his daughter whom you once helped.

Always remember **the most important rule in getting contributions: ask**. When that does not happen, nothing happens. *Success is asking for money. Positive results do occur when you ask using effective methods.*

DIRECT MAIL LETTERS

Direct mail letters, those sent directly to specific persons on a mailing list, are often a central part of the annual campaign. Research repeatedly shows what was mentioned before, that the more personal the approach is, the better the response is. A conversational easy to read style of writing, any handwriting, use of a person's name rather than "Dear Supporters," all these produce more donations. Think of direct mail fund-raising, like all fund-raising, as friend raising.

A typical direct mail letter is a package containing: the appeal letter, a pre-addressed return envelope, a response card to be sent back, and an eye catching enclosure (such as a brochure) that tries to sell the reader a second time on making a gift. Each nonprofit should have a brochure about itself. One purpose of the brochure is to make the case for support. *A brochure will come in handy on many occasions.*

Start strong in the first paragraph with a story or a phrase that arouses interest. Involve and inform the reader. Show the reader how he or she can make a difference. Pick a person to sign the letter who will add impact to the appeal. Use an effective P.S. because that part of the letter often gets special notice.

The letter should include a description of: the need, the people who have the need, the benefits from meeting the need, why your nonprofit is capable of meeting the need, the use of the contribution, and why this contribution is important.

Direct mail campaigns involve several functions: donor targeting, mailing list preparation, database management, writing, design, printing, labeling, mailing, and follow up. Contributions increase when a letter is followed up by a related phone call.

Results depend highly on **how the mailing list has been compiled**. How strong is the already existing connection between the people included on the list and your organization? If the connection is weak, the response will be weak. Buying a commercial list is not a very productive option for the typical local nonprofit. You might trade your mailing list of contributors with another local nonprofit. Studies demonstrate this will not hurt the next financial response you get from your donors.

Sometimes prospecting by using a list of marginal value is productive in the long run. There might be contributions from 2% of the persons contacted. However, the contributions from those responding may pay for your mailing costs, and you can go back year after year to these new proven donors to bring in substantial revenue. The value is in the long-term revenue. An average direct mail response rate to a letter from a nation-wide organization is between 2% to 3%. Your rate can and should be higher.

Using free computer databases available at libraries or through the Internet allows you to locate new addresses for people. Also city directories will indicate who lives at a given address, and his or her phone number.

With letters, as with other fund-raising materials, validate their effectiveness before large-scale use. Do a small-scale test mailing first to see the results from a particular letter, then proceed to a large mailing.

There are many books which describe direct mail specifics and tell you how best to prepare the letters, how to involve the reader in your story, and how to generate more replies. In addition, **save fund-raising mail sent to you** to gather ideas for your own mailings.

TELEPHONE CALLS

All fund-raising is a contact sport. Telephone solicitations are part of the whole fund-raising plan. Often having a special crew of well trained volunteers produces a good return, such as when college students telephone the school alumni. When the executive director of an agency calls, he or she should be looking for a large donation. Many executives dislike making fund-raising calls, but *the calls are essential* for donations. (Cultivation at some point ought to have taken place before the phone call.)

More income is generated when telephone calls are integrated into a larger plan that includes on-going contacts and mailings to prepare a potential donor for the request. Using multiple channels of communication strengthens an appeal.

There are commercial firms which will make the calls for your organization. On average nonprofits that hire solicitation companies receive only about one-third of the total money given.

You know from being on the receiving end that telephone fund-raising can be done badly. Many recipients of the calls are not receptive.

A good script with a few key points is a must. The script should not be rattled off mechanically. Capturing the listener's interest quickly is essential. Try to get the caller involved in a conversation by asking questions. Develop a flow of "yes" answers that lead to a final "yes" when the request to donate is made.

A selective list of phone numbers is important. You could start with persons who receive your newsletter, then move to those who have had any contact with your nonprofit. Picking people at random, such as from a phone book, is the least effective method of developing a list.

SPECIAL EVENTS

Special events include: dinners, dances, concerts, auctions, walk-a-thons, golf matches, etc. Special events may attract new and uncommitted people to the event, and perhaps to your organization. There are people who will attend a special event who might not get involved any other way.

Once they are attracted, try to draw them into an interest in the life of your agency. Events are often more effective as friend raisers than as fund raisers, which is fine. Send free tickets to government office holders, foundation leaders, corporate executives, and possible major donors.

Special events should not just raise funds, but should also cultivate prospective long-term supporters. One of your major objectives is to get people involved, and then move their involvement and commitment up to higher and higher levels. One quick way of phrasing this objective is: "bring 'em in, move 'em up."

Special events present you with fine opportunities for news coverage, and heighten your visibility in the community. However, experienced fund-raisers consistently agree that special events when compared to the other options are not nearly the best financial return for the time and money invested.

Because there are so many details specific to each unique type of special event, I cannot go into the methods to use for each. Let me just say that with all of them you should have (well in advance) a written plan with a budget. The plan states what has to be done, when, by whom. *Persons who possess initiative are vital to promote the event.* How it is advertised and promoted frequently accounts for the difference between a so-so event and a great success.

There are several other fund-raising methods which I will briefly comment upon next. Maybe you can think of specific methods that you have seen used productively.

THE UNITED WAY

United Way support is good source of funding. You may want to contact the United Way if you are not a participant now.

This support will be regular and reliable. You can learn a great deal from their fund-raising techniques. Make your case to the United Way by demonstrating that you are meeting an important community need.

INTERNET SITES

An organization's Internet site can be used to raise funds. The American Red Cross raised $2.5 million through their Internet site in one year. A nonprofit's site may showcase information about the organization, illustrate giving options, solicit gifts and credit card donations, recruit membership, and recognize donors. Include your mission, accomplishments, plans for the future, needs, and a section for volunteering and newsletter sign-up. A web site can be used for a wide variety of creative purposes.

You should keep your appeal brief. Net users tend to scan materials quickly. The net is a method to communicate with a segment of your potential supporters, but not all of them. Many persons just do not use the Internet.

EARNED INCOME

Another fund-raising method is earned income from fees, such as for providing new or current services, offering counseling, or teaching classes. You would be applying your organizational expertise and *using your strengths* to earn income. People will pay for what you can offer them.

You might also produce and sell a product that you are in a unique position to make. Of course most nonprofit organizations are service providers and offering services will be more natural. Check out any plans with your accountant. There may be tax implications from some income producing endeavors.

FRIENDS GROUPS

A friends group, a group of volunteers dedicated to advancing your organization, can be a valuable source of support. A group, such as "Friends of the Rehabilitation Center," provides a pool of volunteers and financial contributors. They can do some of the work of fund-raising for you.

This group of supporting members will make annual contributions and are also likely to remember you in their estate planning. One or two active leaders in the friends group could make the association a self-sustaining asset. Pick some committed supporters and enlist them in building the base of support. They can cultivate more volunteers.

NEWSLETTERS

Distributing a newsletter is a fine way to stay in touch with those who have at some time come into contact with your organization. A regular means of communication will strengthen the ties to your organization's friends and potential friends.

A newsletter of even one page is a way to maintain communication, keep a higher profile, and convince your constituents that your nonprofit is doing good things. Staff and volunteers could contribute articles. You might publish stories on the need for donations or the advantages of planned giving. If your organization holds a raffle or a bake sale, the newsletter could promote sales.

> **Do you see how these fund-raising methods work together**? For instance, special events bring in new donors who will be added to your newsletter mailing list. Your newsletter keeps donors motivated to give. That in turn helps make direct mail for the annual fund more successful. The annual fund list of donors becomes the prospect list for planned gifts and major gifts.

GETTING STARTED

Let me say again that each organization really ought to have a comprehensive long-range financial plan that takes full advantage of its opportunities. The written plan should indicate the goals, the methodology, a timetable for action, a budget, and what personnel time will be required.

If your nonprofit is starting from scratch the financial development methods to begin with are:

- cultivation of potential donors
- a newsletter
- a friends group
- special events
- direct mail and phone calls
- an annual giving program

Here is a web site for those who like the Internet: http://fundclass-digest@fundraiser-software.com. By then going into "FundClass" you can learn online about fund-raising topics.

I have outlined some fund-raising methods for you. To start things moving, **get your C.E.O. to review these methods and to appoint a committee to develop your financial plan**. Involve the board of trustees in the plan. In fact every nonprofit organization should have a permanent active committee of board members who are focused on raising funds. The board has an obligation to provide leadership. For fund-raising to be successful **the board must be committed to the effort**. You could get the board up to speed by giving them all a book that goes into more detail about fund-raising alternatives than this chapter. Then in meetings discuss what they have read. There could be a board retreat on the topic of fund-raising, or guest speakers.

A good overview of raising money is *Fundraising for Social Change* by Kim Klein. Consider reading that or other books on fund-raising to develop your understanding of the subject.

The fund-raising process is lucrative. There are results to take pride in. Being involved makes you look good, and substantially assists your nonprofit in meeting its goal of helping people.

INTERNET SITES FOR GRANT SEEKERS

In getting a grant for a nonprofit organization, the Internet can be a source of information. Federal government grants are covered in detail. Corporate information is available on the net, but is seldom oriented toward grants. Only a small percentage of foundations have web pages, however foundation tax returns can be found on the GrantSmart, GuideStar and Foundation Center web sites. Here are seven good sites.

Catalog of Federal Domestic Assistance
http://www.cfda.gov
The comprehensive database can be searched using keywords to find federal grant programs, and there are also tips on getting federal grants.

Federal Register
http://ocd.usda.gov/nofa.htm
This federal government site indexes and summarizes new grant notices which appear in the Federal Register.

Foundation Center
http://www.fdncenter.org
The Foundation Center site contains information about foundations, corporate grant makers, the Center's resources, philanthropic news, and frequently asked grant questions. The site allows you to check foundation tax returns, the 990-PFs, which are very informative.

Fundsnet Online Services

http://www.fundsnetservices.com

Fundsnet has numerous sections about nonprofit resources, foundations, and fund-raising. See the Grantwriting Resources section.

Grantsmanship Center

http://www.tgci.com

These web pages contain information about the Center, its magazine, grant resources, training classes, and some federal grant proposal abstracts.

GrantSmart

http://www.grantsmart.org

In looking here for a foundation tax return, start under "Search."

GuideStar

http://www.guidestar.org

GuideStar is a service with the tax returns of foundations, background on the programs and finances of more than 700,000 American nonprofit organizations, plus news stories on philanthropy.

INDEX

2-4-8, 102-103
501(c)(3), 17-18
990-PF, 47-49

Annual giving programs, 114-115
Assoc. of Fundraising Professionals, 79

Books of grant sources, 32-45
Budget example, 75

Capital campaigns, 112-113
Catalog of Federal Dom. Assistance,
   36-37, 41-45, 50
Charitable trusts, 109
Checklist, grant, 6-7
Computer resources, 46, 121-122
Cooperating collections, 37
Corporations, 12-14
Cultivation of individual donors, 107

Deadlines, 25, 79
Direct mail, 115-116
Document proposal, 58-61

Feasibility study, 113
Foundation Center cooperating
   collections, 37
Foundation Directory, 30-40, 46
Foundation tax returns, 47-49

Foundations, 10-11
   community foundations, 11
   comparison to federal govt., 26
Funder identification work sheet, 27-28
Funders, best options, 16
Funders, gripes of, 57-58
Fund-raising, getting started, 120

Geographic focus of funders, 23
Government, 14-16
   comparison to foundations, 26
   grants information, 49-50
   proposals, 83-85
Grant checklist, 6-7
Grants, size of, 23-24

Indirect costs, 72-74
Internet sites for grants, 121-122

Letter of inquiry, 52
Letter proposal, 58-60

Mail, direct, 115-116
Major gifts, 110-112

Personal contacts with funders, 51-53
Plan for use of the grant, 2-4
Planned giving, 108-110

Proposal
    appendix, 76-77
    cost, 71-76
    evaluation, 68-70
    goals and benefits, 65-66
    need, 64
    our organization, 62-63
    plan, 66-67
    summary, 62
Proposal example, 90-100
Proposal work sheet, 87-89

Relationships with grant funders, 11
Request for proposals, 18

Shotgun method, 19-20
Size of grants, 23-24
Special events, 117-118
Subject interests of funders, 21-23

Tax returns of foundations, 47-49
Telephone fund-raising calls, 116-117
Trusts, charitable, 109
Types of support, 24-25

Work sheets
    funder identification, 27-28
    proposal, 87-89